Cyrano de Bergerac
by Edmond Rostand

AN HEROIC COMEDY IN
FIVE ACTS

Translated into English Verse
by BRIAN HOOKER

Prepared for WALTER HAMPDEN

W9-AQH-773

BANTAM BOOKS

TORONTO · NEW YORK · LONDON · SYDNEY · AUCKLAND

*This low-priced Bantam Book
has been completely reset in a type face
designed for easy reading, and was printed
from new plates. It contains the complete
text of the original hard-cover edition.*
NOT ONE WORD HAS BEEN OMITTED.

CYRANO DE BERGERAC

*A Bantam Book / published by arrangement with
Holt, Rinehart & Winston, Inc.*

PRINTING HISTORY
Cyrano de Bergerac was first performed in 1898.
First Bantam publication / October 1950
Bantam Classic Edition / March 1981
2nd printing . . . August 1982
3rd printing . . . December 1982

Cover art courtesy of the Bettman Archives.

*Cover photo of Cyrano de Bergerac as
portrayed by José Ferrer.*

All rights reserved.
Copyright 1923 by Henry Holt and Company.
Copyright 1951 by Doris C. Hooker.
*This book may not be reproduced in whole or in part, by
mimeograph or any other means, without permission.
For information address: Bantam Books, Inc.*

ISBN 0-553-21118-8

Published simultaneously in the United States and Canada

PRINTED IN THE UNITED STATES OF AMERICA

O   12 11 10 9 8 7 6 5

EDMOND ROSTAND

was born in Marseilles in 1868 and died in 1918. His thirty-year literary career is marked primarily by one astronomical success and a number of plays of lesser note. His father, Eugene Rostand, a poet, economist and scholar, had groomed Edmond for a career as a lawyer. Early on, however, he displayed an interest in marionette theater and poetry. While attending the Collège Stanislas in Paris, Rostand studied French literature, history and philosophy. He followed his own inclinations and deviated from the course designed for him, although he did finally earn a legal degree and gain admission to the bar. His first poetry appeared in the small academy review *Mireille*. In 1888, his *Le Gant Rouge* was produced and, in 1890, Rostand published his first book of poetry, *Les Musardises*. His play *Les Romanesques* (*The Romancers*) was produced in 1894, followed a year later by *La Princesse Lointaine* (*Princess Faraway*). The playwright's name and influence spread. Popular stars of the theater, including Sarah Bernhardt and Benoît Constant Coquelin, were featured in the most prominent roles.

Rostand's fame peaked in 1898 with the first production of *Cyrano de Bergerac*, a five-act verse drama. The play was important to the drama of its time for its romantic nature, a departure from the realistic conventions then in vogue. It was an enormous success.

After his next success, *L'Aiglon* (*The Eaglet*) (1900), ten years followed before Rostand completed another play. *Chantecler*, an allegorical, experimental drama, opened in 1910 and was quickly judged a failure.

Rostand was refused entrance into the French Army in 1914 because of his failing health. He spent the remaining years of his life in semiretirement. His final play *La Dernière Nuit de Don Juan* (*The Last Night of Don Juan*), opened in 1922, four years after his death, and received no better response than had *Chantecler*.

Bantam Classics
Ask your bookseller for these other World Classics

GREEK DRAMA, edited by Moses Hadas
THE COMPLETE PLAYS OF SOPHOCLES
TEN PLAYS, Euripides
THE COMPLETE PLAYS OF ARISTOPHANES
PLAUTUS: THREE COMEDIES (translated by Erich Segal)
THE AENEID, Virgil (translated by Allen Mandelbaum)
INFERNO, Dante (translated by Allen Mandelbaum)
PURGATORIO, Dante (translated by Allen Mandelbaum)
THE PRINCE, Machiavelli
CANDIDE, Voltaire
THE COUNT OF MONTE CRISTO, Alexandre Dumas
THE THREE MUSKETEERS, Alexandre Dumas
THE HUNCHBACK OF NOTRE DAME, Victor Hugo
MADAME BOVARY, Gustave Flaubert
FATHERS AND SONS, Ivan Turgenev
ANNA KARENINA, Leo Tolstoy
THE DEATH OF IVAN ILYICH, Leo Tolstoy
THE BROTHERS KARAMAZOV, Fyodor Dostoevsky
CRIME AND PUNISHMENT, Fyodor Dostoevsky
THE IDIOT, Fyodor Dostoevsky
NOTES FROM UNDERGROUND, Fyodor Dostoevsky
CYRANO DE BERGERAC, Edmond Rostand
20,000 LEAGUES UNDER THE SEA, Jules Verne
AROUND THE WORLD IN EIGHTY DAYS, Jules Verne
FOUR GREAT PLAYS, Henrik Ibsen
FIVE MAJOR PLAYS, Anton Chekhov
THE METAMORPHOSIS, Franz Kafka

It was to the soul of CYRANO *that I intended to dedicate this poem.*

But since that soul has been reborn in you, COQUELIN, *it is to you that I dedicate it.*

E. R.

THE PERSONS

Cyrano de Bergerac

Christian de Neuvillette

Comte de Guiche

Ragueneau

Le Bret

Carbon de Castel-Jaloux

The Cadets

Lignière

Vicomte de Valvert

A Marquis

Second Marquis

Third Marquis

Montfleury

Bellerose

Jodelet

Cuigy

Brissaille

A Meddler

A Musketeer

Another Musketeer

A Spanish Officer

A Cavalier

The Porter

A Citizen

His Son

A Cut-Purse

A Spectator

A Sentry

Bertrandou the Fifer

A Capuchin

Two Musicians

The Poets

The Pastrycooks

The Pages

Roxane

Her Duenna

Lise

The Orange Girl

Mother Marguérite de Jesus

Sister Marthe

Sister Claire

An Actress

A Soubrette

The Flower Girl

The Crowd, Citizens, Marquis, Musketeers, Thieves, Pastrycooks, Poets, Cadets of Gascoyne, Actors, Violins, Pages, Children, Spanish Soldiers, Spectators, Intellectuals, Academicians, Nuns, etc.

(The first four Acts in 1640; the fifth in 1655.)

FIRST ACT: A Performance at the Hotel de Bourgogne.

SECOND ACT: The Bakery of the Poets.

THIRD ACT: Roxane's Kiss.

FOURTH ACT: The Cadets of Gascoyne.

FIFTH ACT: Cyrano's Gazette.

THE FIRST ACT

THE HALL OF THE HÔTEL DE BOURGOGNE in 1640. *A sort of Tennis Court, arranged and decorated for Theatrical productions.*

The Hall is a long rectangle; we see it diagonally, in such a way that one side of it forms the back scene, which begins at the First Entrance on the Right and runs up to the Last Entrance on the Left, where it makes a right angle with the Stage which is seen obliquely.

This Stage is provided on either hand with benches placed along the wings. The curtain is formed by two lengths of Tapestry which can be drawn apart. Above a Harlequin cloak, the Royal Arms. Broad steps lead from the Stage down to the floor of the Hall. On either side of these steps, a place for the Musicians. A row of candles serving as footlights. Two tiers of Galleries along the side of the Hall; the upper one divided into boxes.

There are no seats upon the Floor, which is the actual stage of our theatre; but toward the back of the Hall, on the right, a few benches are arranged; and underneath a stairway on the extreme right, which leads up to the galleries, and of which only the lower portion is visible, there is a sort of Sideboard, decorated with little tapers, vases of flowers, bottles and glasses, plates of cake, et cetera.

Farther along, toward the centre of our stage is the Entrance to the Hall; a great double door which opens only slightly to admit the Audience. On one of the panels of this door, as also in other places about the Hall, and in particular just over the Sideboard, are Playbills in red, upon which we may read the title LA CLORISE.

As the CURTAIN RISES, the Hall is dimly lighted and still empty. The Chandeliers are lowered to the floor, in the middle of the Hall, ready for lighting.

> *(Sound of voices outside the door. Then a Cavalier enters abruptly.)*

THE PORTER
(Follows him)

Halloa there!—Fifteen sols!

THE CAVALIER

I enter free.

THE PORTER

Why?

THE CAVALIER

Soldier of the Household of the King!

THE PORTER
(Turns to another Cavalier who has just entered)

You?

SECOND CAVALIER

I pay nothing.

THE PORTER

Why not?

SECOND CAVALIER

Musketeer!

FIRST CAVALIER
(To the Second)

The play begins at two. Plenty of time—
And here's the whole floor empty. Shall we try
Our exercise?

(They fence with the foils which they have brought)

A LACKEY
(Enters)

—Pst! . . . Flanquin! . . .

ANOTHER
(Already on stage)

What, Champagne?

FIRST LACKEY
(Showing games which he takes out of his doublet)

Cards. Dice. Come on.

(Sits on the floor)

SECOND LACKEY
(Same action)

Come on, old cock!

FIRST LACKEY
*(Takes from his pocket a bit of candle, lights it, sets
it on the floor)*

I have stolen

A little of my master's fire.

A GUARDSMAN
(To a flower girl who comes forward)

How sweet

Of you, to come before they light the hall!
> *(Puts his arm around her)*

> #### FIRST CAVALIER
> *(Receives a thrust of the foil)*

A hit!

> #### SECOND LACKEY
> A club!

> #### THE GUARDSMAN
> *(Pursuing the girl)*
>> A kiss!

> #### THE FLOWER GIRL
> *(Pushing away from him)*
>>> They'll see us!—

> #### THE GUARDSMAN
> *(Draws her into a dark corner)*
>>>> No danger!

> #### A MAN
> *(Sits on the floor, together with several others who have brought packages of food)*

When we come early, we have time to eat.

> #### A CITIZEN
> *(Escorting his son, a boy of sixteen)*

Sit here, my son.

> #### FIRST LACKEY
>> Mark the Ace!

> #### ANOTHER MAN
> *(Draws a bottle from under his cloak and sits down with the others)*
>>> Here's the spot

For a jolly old sot to suck his Burgundy—
> *(Drinks)*

Here—in the house of the Burgundians!

> #### THE CITIZEN
> *(To his son)*

Would you not think you were in some den of vice?
> *(Points with his cane at the drunkard)*

Drunkards—
> *(In stepping back, one of the cavaliers trips him up)*
>> Bullies!—

> *(He falls between the lackeys)*
>> Gamblers!—

> #### THE GUARDSMAN
> *(Behind him as he rises, still struggling with the Flower Girl)*
>>> One kiss—

3

Good God!—

(Draws his son quickly away)
Here!—And to think, my son, that in this hall
They play Rotrou!

THE BOY
Yes father—and Corneille!

THE PAGES
(Dance in, holding hands and singing:)
Tra-la-la-la-la-la-la-la-la-la-lère . . .

THE PORTER
You pages there—no nonsense!

FIRST PAGE
(With wounded dignity)
Oh, monsieur!

Really! How could you?
*(To the Second, the moment the Porter turns his
back)*
Pst!—a bit of string?

SECOND PAGE
(Shows fishline with hook)
Yes—and a hook.

FIRST PAGE
Up in the gallery,

And fish for wigs!

A CUT-PURSE
*(Gathers around him several evil-looking young
fellows)*
Now then, you picaroons,
Perk up, and hear me mutter. Here's your bout—
Bustle around some cull, and bite his bung . . .

SECOND PAGE
(Calls to other pages already in the gallery)
Hey! Brought your pea-shooters?

THIRD PAGE
(From above)
And our peas, too!

(Blows, and showers them with peas)
THE BOY
What is the play this afternoon?

THE CITIZEN
"Clorise."

THE BOY
Who wrote that?

4

> Balthasar Baro. What a play! . . .
> *(He takes the Boy's arm and leads him upstage)*

THE CUT-PURSE
(To his pupils)

Lace now, on those long sleeves, you cut it off—
> *(Gesture with thumb and finger, as if using scissors)*

A SPECTATOR
(To another, pointing upward toward the gallery)

Ah, *Le Cid!*—Yes, the first night, I sat there—

THE CUT-PURSE

Watches—
> *(Gesture as of picking a pocket)*

THE CITIZEN
(Coming down with his son)
> Great actors we shall see to-day—

THE CUT-PURSE

Handkerchiefs—
> *(Gesture of holding the pocket with left hand, and
> drawing out handkerchief with right)*

THE CITIZEN
> Montfleury—

A VOICE
(In the gallery)

> Lights! Light the lights!

THE CITIZEN

Bellerose, l'Épy, Beaupre, Jodelet—

A PAGE
(On the floor)

Here comes the orange girl.

THE ORANGE GIRL

> Oranges, milk,

Raspberry syrup, lemonade—
> *(Noise at the door)*

A FALSETTO VOICE
(Outside)

> Make way,

Brutes!

FIRST LACKEY
> What, the Marquis—on the floor?
> *(The Marquis enter in a little group.)*

SECOND LACKEY

> Not long—

Only a few moments; they'll go and sit

On the stage presently.

FIRST MARQUIS
(Seeing the hall half empty)

How now! We enter
Like tradespeople—no crowding, no disturbance !—
No treading on the toes of citizens?
Oh fie! Oh fie!
*(He encounters two gentlemen who have already
arrived)*

Cuigy! Brissaille!
(Great embracings)

CUIGY

The faithful!

(Looks around him.)
We are here before the candles.

FIRST MARQUIS

Ah, be still!

You put me in a temper.

SECOND MARQUIS

Console yourself,

Marquis—The lamplighter!

THE CROWD
(Applauding the appearance of the lamplighter)

Ah! . . .

*(A group gathers around the chandelier while he
lights it. A few people have already taken their
place in the gallery. LIGNIÈRE enters the hall,
arm in arm with CHRISTIAN DE NEUVILLETTE.
LIGNIÈRE is a slightly disheveled figure, dissi-
pated and yet distinguished looking. CHRISTIAN,
elegantly but rather unfashionably dressed, appears preoccupied and keeps looking up at the
boxes.)*

CUIGY

Lignière!—

BRISSAILLE
(Laughing)
Still sober—at this hour?

LIGNIÈRE
(To CHRISTIAN)

May I present you?

(CHRISTIAN assents.)
Baron Christian de Neuvillette.
(They salute.)

6

THE CROWD
(Applauding as the lighted chandelier is hoisted into place)

Ah!—

CUIGY
(Aside to BRISSAILLE, looking at CHRISTIAN)

Rather

A fine head, is it not? The profile . . .

FIRST MARQUIS
(Who has overheard)

Peuh!

LIGNIÈRE
(Presenting them to CHRISTIAN)
Messieurs de Cuigy . . . de Brissaille . . .

CHRISTIAN
(Bows)

Enchanted!

FIRST MARQUIS
(To the second)
He is not ill-looking; possibly a shade
Behind the fashion.

LIGNIÈRE
(To CUIGY)

Monsieur is recently

From the Touraine.

CHRISTIAN

Yes, I have been in Paris
Two or three weeks only. I join the Guards
To-morrow.

FIRST MARQUIS
(Watching the people who come into the boxes)
Look—Madame la Présidente

Aubry!

THE ORANGE GIRL
Oranges, milk—
THE VIOLINS
(Tuning up)
La . . . la . . .
CUIGY
(To CHRISTIAN, calling his attention to the increasing crowd)

We have

An audience to-day!

CHRISTIAN
A brilliant one.

FIRST MARQUIS

Oh yes, all our own people—the gay world!

> *(They name the ladies who enter the boxes elaborately dressed. Bows and smiles are exchangéd.)*

SECOND MARQUIS

Madame de Guéméné . . .

CUIGY

De Bois-Dauphin . . .

FIRST MARQUIS

Whom we adore—

BRISSAILLE

Madame de Chavigny . . .

SECOND MARQUIS

Who plays with all our hearts—

LIGNIÈRE

Why, there's Corneille

Returned from Rouen!

THE BOY

> *(To his father)*

Are the Academy

All here?

THE CITIZEN

I see some of them . . . there's Boudu—
Boissat—Cureau—Porchères—Colomby—
Bourzeys—Bourdon—Arbaut—

Ah, those great names,

Never to be forgotten!

FIRST MARQUIS

Look—at last!

Our Intellectuals! Barthénoide,
Urimédonte, Félixérie . . .

SECOND MARQUIS

> *(Languishing)*

Sweet heaven!

How exquisite their surnames are! Marquis,
You know them all?

FIRST MARQUIS

I know them all, Marquis!

LIGNIÈRE

> *(Draws* CHRISTIAN *aside)*

My dear boy, I came here to serve you— Well,
But where's the lady? I'll be going.

CHRISTIAN

Not yet—

8

A little longer! She is always here.
Please! I must find some way of meeting her.
I am dying of love! And you—you know
Everyone, the whole court and the whole town,
And put them all into your songs—at least
You can tell me her name!

THE FIRST VIOLIN
(Raps on his desk with his bow)

Pst— Gentlemen!

(Raises his bow)
THE ORANGE GIRL

Macaroons, lemonade—

CHRISTIAN

Then she may be
One of those æsthetes . . . Intellectuals,
You call them— How can I talk to a woman
In that style? I have no wit. This fine manner
Of speaking and of writing nowadays—
Not for me! I am a soldier—and afraid.
That's her box, on the right—the empty one.

LIGNIÈRE
(Starts for the door)

I am going.

CHRISTIAN
(Restrains him)
No—wait!

LIGNIÈRE

Not I. There's a tavern
Not far away—and I am dying of thirst.

THE ORANGE GIRL
(Passes with her tray)

Orange juice?

LIGNIÈRE

No!

THE ORANGE GIRL
Milk?

LIGNIÈRE

Pouah!

THE ORANGE GIRL

Muscatel?

LIGNIÈRE

Here! Stop!
(To CHRISTIAN)
I'll stay a little.

(To the Girl)

Let me see

Your Muscatel.

(He sits down by the sideboard. The Girl pours out wine for him.)

VOICES

(In the crowd about the door, upon the entrance of a spruce little man, rather fat, with a beaming smile)

Ragueneau!

LIGNIÈRE

(To CHRISTIAN*)*

Ragueneau,

Poet and pastry-cook—a character!

RAGUENEAU

(Dressed like a confectioner in his Sunday clothes, advances quickly to LIGNIÈRE*)*

Sir, have you seen Monsieur de Cyrano?

LIGNIÈRE

(Presents him to CHRISTIAN*)*

Permit me . . . Ragueneau, confectioner,
The chief support of modern poetry.

RAGUENEAU

(Bridling)

Oh—too much honor!

LIGNIÈRE

Patron of the Arts—

Mæcenas! Yes, you are—

RAGUENEAU

Undoubtedly,

The poets gather round my hearth.

LIGNIÈRE

On credit—

Himself a poet—

RAGUENEAU

So they say—

LIGNIÈRE

Maintains

The Muses.

RAGUENEAU

It is true that for an ode—

LIGNIÈRE

You give a tart—

RAGUENEAU

A tartlet—

10

LIGNIÈRE

.Modesty!

And for a triolet you give—

RAGUENEAU

Plain bread.

LIGNIÈRE

(Severely)

Bread and milk! And you love the theatre?

RAGUENEAU

I adore it!

LIGNIÈRE

Well, pastry pays for all.
Your place to-day now— Come, between ourselves,
What did it cost you?

RAGUENEAU

Four pies; fourteen cakes.

(Looking about)

But— Cyrano not here? Astonishing!

LIGNIÈRE

Why so?

RAGUENEAU

Why— Montfleury plays!

LIGNIÈRE

Yes, I hear

That hippopotamus assumes the rôle
Of Phédon. What is that to Cyrano?

RAGUENEAU

Have you not heard? Monsieur de Bergerac
So hates Montfleury, he has forbidden him
For three weeks to appear upon the stage.

LIGNIÈRE

(Who is, by this time, at his fourth glass)

Well?

RAGUENEAU

Montfleury plays!—

CUIGY

(Strolls over to them)

Yes—what then?

RAGUENEAU

Ah! That

Is what I came to see.

FIRST MARQUIS

This Cyrano—

Who is he?

CUIGY

Oh, he is the lad with the long sword.

SECOND MARQUIS

Noble?

CUIGY

Sufficiently; he is in the Guards.
*(Points to a gentleman who comes and goes about
the hall as though seeking for someone)*
His friend Le Bret can tell you more.
(Calls to him)

Le Bret!

(LE BRET comes down to them)
Looking for Bergerac?

LE BRET

Yes. And for trouble

CUIGY

Is he not an extraordinary man?

LE BRET

The best friend and the bravest soul alive!

RAGUENEAU

Poet—

CUIGY

Swordsman—

LE BRET

Musician—

BRISSAILLE

Philosopher—

LIGNIÈRE

Such a remarkable appearance, too!

RAGUENEAU

Truly, I should not look to find his portrait
By the grave hand of Philippe de Champagne.
He might have been a model for Callot—
One of those wild swashbucklers in a masque—
Hat with three plumes, and doublet with six points—
His cloak behind him over his long sword
Cocked, like the tail of strutting Chanticleer—
Prouder than all the swaggering Tamburlaines
Hatched out of Gascony. And to complete
This Punchinello figure—such a nose!—
My lords, there is no such nose as that nose—
You cannot look upon it without crying: "Oh, no,
Impossible! Exaggerated!" Then
You smile, and say: "Of course— I might have known;
Presently he will take it off." But that

12

Monsieur de Bergerac will never do.

LIGNIÈRE

(Grimly)

He keeps it—and God help the man who smiles!

RAGUENEAU

His sword is one half of the shears of Fate!

FIRST MARQUIS

(Shrugs)

He will not come.

RAGUENEAU

       Will he not? Sir, I'll lay you
A pullet à la Ragueneau!

FIRST MARQUIS

(Laughing)

     Done!
(Murmurs of admiration; ROXANE has just appeared in her box. She sits at the front of the box, and her Duenna takes a seat toward the rear. CHRISTIAN, busy paying the Orange Girl, does not see her at first.)

SECOND MARQUIS

(With little excited cries)

          Ah!
Oh! Oh! Sweet sirs, look yonder! Is she not
Frightfully ravishing?

FIRST MARQUIS

       Bloom of the peach—
Blush of the strawberry—

SECOND MARQUIS

        So fresh—so cool,
That our hearts, grown all warm with loving her,
May catch their death of cold!

CHRISTIAN

(Looks up, sees ROXANE, and seizes LIGNIÈRE by the arm.)

       There! Quick—up there—
In the box! Look!—

LIGNIÈRE

(Coolly)

   Herself?

CHRISTIAN

       Quickly— Her name?

LIGNIÈRE

(Sipping his wine, and speaking between sips)

Madeleine Robin, called Roxane . . . refined . . .
Intellectual . . .

CHRISTIAN

Ah!—

LIGNIÈRE

Unmarried . . .

CHRISTIAN

Oh!—

LIGNIÈRE

No title . . . rich enough . . . an orphan . . . cousin
To Cyrano . . . of whom we spoke just now . . .
*(At this point, a very distinguished looking gentle-
man, the Cordon Bleu around his neck, enters
the box, and stands a moment talking with
ROXANE.)*

CHRISTIAN

(Starts)
And the man? . . .

LIGNIÈRE

*(Beginning to feel his wine a little; cocks his eye
at them.)*

Oho! That man? . . . Comte de Guiche . . .
In love with her . . . married himself, however,
To the niece of the Cardinal—Richelieu . . .
Wishes Roxane, therefore, to marry one
Monsieur de Valvert . . . Vicomte . . . friend of his . . .
A somewhat melancholy gentleman . . .
But . . . well, accommodating! . . . She says No . . .
Nevertheless, de Guiche is powerful . . .
Not above persecuting . . .
(He rises, swaying a little, and very happy.)

I have written

A little song about his little game . . .
Good little song, too . . . Here, I'll sing it for you . . .
Make de Guiche furious . . . naughty little song . . .
Not so bad, either— Listen! . . .
(He stands with his glass held aloft, ready to sing.)

CHRISTIAN

No. Adieu.

LIGNIÈRE

Whither away?

CHRISTIAN

To Monsieur de Valvert!

LIGNIÈRE

Careful! The man's a swordsman . . .
*(Nods toward ROXANE, who is watching CHRIS-
TIAN.)*

14

Looking at you—

Wait! Someone

CHRISTIAN

Roxane! . . .

*(He forgets everything, and stands spellbound, gaz-
ing toward ROXANE. The Cut-Purse and his
crew, observing him transfixed, his eyes raised
and his mouth half open, begin edging in his
direction.)*

LIGNIÈRE

Oh! Very well,

Then I'll be leaving you . . . Good day . . . Good day! . . .

(CHRISTIAN remains motionless.)

Everywhere else, they like to hear me sing!—
Also, I am thirsty.

*(He goes out, navigating carefully. LE BRET, hav-
ing made the circuit of the hall, returns to RA-
GUENEAU, somewhat reassured.)*

LE BRET

No sign anywhere

Of Cyrano!

RAGUENEAU

(Incredulous)

Wait and see!

LE BRET

Humph! I hope

He has not seen the bill.

THE CROWD

The play!— The play!—

FIRST MARQUIS

*(Observing DE GUICHE, as he descends from ROX-
ANE'S box and crosses the floor, followed by a
knot of obsequious gentlemen, the VICOMTE DE
VALVERT among them.)*

This man de Guiche—what ostentation!

SECOND MARQUIS

Bah!—

Another Gascon!

FIRST MARQUIS

Gascon, yes—but cold

And calculating—certain to succeed—
My word for it. Come, shall we make our bow?
We shall be none the worse, I promise you . . .

(They go toward DE GUICHE.)

SECOND MARQUIS

Beautiful ribbons, Count! That color, now,
What is it—"Kiss-me-Dear" or "Startled-Fawn"?

DE GUICHE

I call that shade "The Dying Spaniard."

FIRST MARQUIS

Ha!

And no false colors either—thanks to you
And your brave troops, in Flanders before long
The Spaniard will die daily.

DE GUICHE

Shall we go

And sit upon the stage? Come, Valvert.

CHRISTIAN

(Starts at the name)

Valvert!—

The Vicomte— Ah, that scoundrel! Quick—my glove—
I'll throw it in his face—

*(Reaching into his pocket for his glove, he catches
the hand of the Cut-Purse)*

THE CUT-PURSE

Oh!—

CHRISTIAN

(Holding fast to the man's wrist)

Who are you?

I was looking for a glove—

THE CUT-PURSE

(Cringing)

You found a hand.

(Hurriedly)

Let me go— I can tell you something—

CHRISTIAN

(Still holding him)

Well?

THE CUT-PURSE

Lignière—that friend of yours—

CHRISTIAN

(Same business)

Well?

THE CUT-PURSE

Good as dead—

Understand? Ambuscaded. Wrote a song
About—no matter. There's a hundred men

16

Waiting for him to-night—I'm one of them.

CHRISTIAN

A hundred? Who arranged this?

THE CUT-PURSE

Secret.

CHRISTIAN

Oh!

THE CUT-PURSE

(With dignity)

Professional secret.

CHRISTIAN

Where are they to be?

THE CUT-PURSE

Porte de Nesle. On his way home. Tell him so.
Save his life.

CHRISTIAN

(Releases the man)

Yes, but where am I to find him?

THE CUT-PURSE

Go round the taverns. There's the Golden Grape,
The Pineapple, the Bursting Belt, the Two
Torches, the Three Funnels—in every one
You leave a line of writing—understand?
To warn him.

CHRISTIAN

(Starts for the door)

I'll go! God, what swine—a hundred

Against one man! . . .

(Stops and looks longingly at ROXANE*)*

Leave *her* here!—

(Savagely, turning toward VALVERT*)*

And leave *him!*—

(Decidedly)

I must save Lignière!

(Exit)

*(DE GUICHE, VALVERT, and all the Marquis have
disappeared through the curtains, to take their
seats upon the stage. The floor is entirely filled;
not a vacant seat remains in the gallery or in
the boxes.)*

THE CROWD

The play! The play!

Begin the play!

17

A CITIZEN
*(As his wig is hoisted into the air on the end of a
fishline, in the hands of a page in the gallery)*
My wig!!

CRIES OF JOY

He's bald! Bravo,
You pages! Ha ha ha!

THE CITIZEN
(Furious, shakes his fist at the boy)
Here, you young villain!

CRIES OF LAUGHTER
(Beginning very loud, then suddenly repressed)
HA HA! Ha Ha! ha ha . . .
(Complete silence)

LE BRET
(Surprised)

That sudden hush? . . .
(A Spectator whispers in his ear.)
Yes?

THE SPECTATOR
I was told on good authority . . .

MURMURS
(Here and there)
What? . . . Here? . . . No . . . Yes . . . Look—in the latticed
box—
The Cardinal! . . . The Cardinal! . . .

A PAGE

The Devil!—
Now we shall all have to behave ourselves!
*(Three raps on the stage. The audience becomes
motionless. Silence)*

THE VOICE OF A MARQUIS
(From the stage, behind the curtains)
Snuff that candle!

ANOTHER MARQUIS
(Puts his head out through the curtains.)
A chair! . . .
*(A chair is passed from hand to hand over the
heads of the crowd. He takes it, and disappears
behind the curtains, not without having blown a
few kisses to the occupants of the boxes.)*

A SPECTATOR

Silence!

VOICES

Hssh! . . . Hssh! . . .

18

(Again the three raps on the stage. The curtains part. TABLEAU. *The Marquis seated on their chairs to right and left of the stage, insolently posed. Back drop representing a pastoral scene, bluish in tone. Four little crystal chandeliers light up the stage. The violins play softly.)*

LE BRET

(In a low tone, to RAGUENEAU)

Montfleury enters now?

RAGUENEAU

(Nods)

Opens the play.

LE BRET

(Much relieved)

Then Cyrano is not here!

RAGUENEAU

I lose . . .

LE BRET

Humph!—

So much the better!

(The melody of a Musette is heard. MONTFLEURY *appears upon the scene, a ponderous figure in the costume of a rustic shepherd, a hat garlanded with roses tilted over one ear, playing upon a beribboned pastoral pipe)*

THE CROWD

(Applauds)

Montfleury! . . . Bravo! . . .

MONTFLEURY

(After bowing to the applause, begins the rôle of Phédon)

"Thrice happy he who hides from pomp and power
In sylvan shade or solitary bower;
Where balmy zephyrs fan his burning cheeks—"

A VOICE

(From the midst of the hall)

Wretch. Have I not forbade you these three weeks?

(Sensation. Everyone turns to look. Murmurs)

SEVERAL VOICES

What? . . . Where? . . . Who is it? . . .

CUIGY

Cyrano!

LE BRET

(In alarm)

Himself!

19

THE VOICE

King of clowns! Leave the stage—*at once!*

THE CROWD

Oh!—

MONTFLEURY

Now,

Now, now—

THE VOICE
You disobey me?

SEVERAL VOICES
(From the floor, from the boxes)

Hsh! Go on—

Quiet!—Go on, Montfleury!—Who's afraid?—

MONTFLEURY
(In a voice of no great assurance)

"Thrice happy he who hides from . . ."

THE VOICE
(More menacingly)

Well? Well? Well? . . .

Monarch of mountebanks! Must I come and plant
A forest on your shoulders?

*(A cane at the end of a long arm shakes above the
heads of the crowd.)*

MONTFLEURY
(In a voice increasingly feeble)

"Thrice hap—"

(The cane is violently agitated.)

THE VOICE

GO!!!

THE CROWD
Ah . . .

CYRANO
*(Arises in the centre of the floor, erect upon a chair,
his arms folded, his hat cocked ferociously, his
moustache bristling, his nose terrible.)*

Presently I shall grow angry!
(Sensation at his appearance)

MONTFLEURY
(To the Marquis)

Messieurs,

If you protect me—

A MARQUIS
(Nonchalantly)

Well—proceed!

20

CYRANO

Fat swine!

If you dare breathe one balmy zephyr more,
I'll fan your cheeks for you!

THE MARQUIS

Quiet down there!

CYRANO

Unless these gentlemen retain their seats,
My cane may bite their ribbons!

ALL THE MARQUIS
(On their feet)

That will do!—

Montfleury—

CYRANO

Fly, goose! Shoo! Take to your wings,
Before I pluck your plumes, and draw your gorge!

A VOICE

See here—

CYRANO

Off stage!!

ANOTHER VOICE

One moment—

CYRANO

What—still there?
(Turns back his cuffs deliberately.)
Very good—then I enter—*Left—with knife*—
To carve this large Italian sausage.

MONTFLEURY
(Desperately attempting dignity)

Sir,

When you insult me, you insult the Muse!

CYRANO
(With great politeness)

Sir, if the Muse, who never knew your name,
Had the honor to meet you—then be sure
That after one glance at that face of yours,
That figure of a mortuary urn—
She would apply her buskin—toward the rear!

THE CROWD

Montfleury! . . . Montfleury! . . . The play! The play!

CYRANO
(To those who are shouting and crowding about him)

Pray you, be gentle with my scabbard here—
She'll put her tongue out at you presently!—

(The circle enlarges.)

THE CROWD

(Recoiling)

Keep back—

CYRANO

(To MONTFLEURY)
            Begone !

THE CROWD

(Pushing in closer, and growling.)
                    Ahr ! . . . ahr ! . . .

CYRANO

(Turns upon them.)

                    Did someone speak?

(They recoil again.)

A VOICE

(In the back of the hall, sings.)
            Monsieur de Cyrano
                Must be another Caesar—
            Let Brutus lay him low,
                And play us "La Clorise" !

ALL THE CROWD

(Singing)
            "La Clorise !" "La Clorise !"

CYRANO

Let me hear one more word of that same song,
And I destroy you all !

A CITIZEN

                Who might you be?

Samson?—

CYRANO

                Precisely. Would you kindly lend me

Your jawbone?

A LADY

(In one of the boxes)
            What an outrage !

A NOBLE

                        Scandalous !

A CITIZEN

Annoying !

A PAGE

            What a game !

THE CROWD

                        Kss ! Montfleury !

Cyrano !

CYRANO

Silence!

THE CROWD

(Delirious)

Woof! Woof! Baaa! Cockadoo!

CYRANO

I—

A PAGE

Meow!

CYRANO

I say be silent!—
(His voice dominates the uproar. Momentary hush.)
And I offer
One universal challenge to you all!
Approach, young heroes—I will take your names.
Each in his turn—no crowding! One, two, three—
Come, get your numbers—who will head the list—
You sir? No— You? Ah, no. To the first man
Who falls I'll build a monument! . . . Not one?
Will all who wish to die, please raise their hands? . . .
I see. You are so modest, you might blush
Before a sword naked. Sweet innocence! . . .
Not one name? Not one finger? . . . Very well,
Then I go on:
(Turning back towards the stage, where MONT-
FLEURY *waits in despair.)*
I'd have our theatre cured
Of this carbuncle. Or if not, why then—
(His hand on his sword hilt.)
The lancet!

MONTFLEURY

I—

CYRANO

*(Descends from his chair, seats himself comfortably
in the centre of the circle which has formed
around him, and makes himself quite at home.)*
Attend to me—full moon!
I clap my hands, three times—thus. At the third
You will eclipse yourself.

THE CROWD

(Amused)

Ah!

CYRANO

Ready? One!

23

MONTFLEURY

I—

A VOICE

(From the boxes)

No!

THE CROWD

He'll go— He'll stay—

MONTFLEURY

I really think,

Gentlemen—

CYRANO

Two!

MONTFLEURY

Perhaps I had better—

CYRANO

Three!

(MONTFLEURY disappears, as if through a trapdoor. Tempest of laughter, hoots and hisses.)

THE CROWD

Yah!—Coward— Come back—

CYRANO

(Beaming, drops back in his chair and crosses his legs)

Let him—if he dare!

A CITIZEN

The Manager! Speech! Speech!

(BELLEROSE advances and bows.)

THE BOXES

Ah! Bellerose!

BELLEROSE

(With elegance)

Most noble—most fair—

THE CROWD

No! The Comedian—

Jodelet!—

JODELET

(Advances, and speaks through his nose.)

Lewd fellows of the baser sort—

THE CROWD

Ha! Ha! Not bad! Bravo!

JODELET

No Bravos here!

Our heavy tragedian with the voluptuous bust

Was taken suddenly—

24

THE CROWD

Yah! Coward!

JODELET

I mean . . .

He had to be excused—

THE CROWD

Call him back— No!—
Yes!—

THE BOY

(To CYRANO*)*

After all, Monsieur, what reason have you
To hate this Montfleury?

CYRANO

(Graciously, still seated)

My dear young man,
I have two reasons, either one alone
Conclusive. *Primo:* A lamentable actor,
Who mouths his verse and moans his tragedy,
And heaves up— Ugh!—like a hod-carrier, lines
That ought to soar on their own wings. *Secundo:*—
Well—that's my secret.

THE OLD CITIZEN

(Behind him)

But you close the play—
"La Clorise"—by Baro! Are we to miss
Our entertainment, merely—

CYRANO

(Respectfully, turns his chair toward the old man)

My dear old boy,
The poetry of Baro being worth
Zero, or less, I feel that I have done
Poetic justice!

THE INTELLECTUALS

(In the boxes)

Really!—our Baro!—
My dear!—Who ever?—Ah, dieu! The idea!—

CYRANO

(Gallantly, turns his chair toward the boxes)

Fair ladies—shine upon us like the sun,
Blossom like the flowers around us—be our songs,
Heard in a dream— Make sweet the hour of death,
Smiling upon us as you close our eyes—
Inspire, but do not try to criticise!

25

Quite so!—and the mere money—possibly
You would like that returned— Yes?

CYRANO

Bellerose,

You speak the first word of intelligence!
I will not wound the mantle of the Muse—
Here, catch!—
(Throws him a purse)
And hold your tongue.

THE CROWD
(Astonished)

Ah! Ah!

JODELET
(Deftly catches the purse, weighs it in his hand.)

Monsieur,

You are hereby authorized to close our play
Every night, on the same terms.

THE CROWD

Boo!

JODELET

And welcome!

Let us be booed together, you and I!

BELLEROSE

Kindly pass out quietly . . .

JODELET
(Burlesquing BELLEROSE)

Quietly . . .

*(They begin to go out, while CYRANO looks about
him with satisfaction. But the exodus ceases presently during the ensuing scene. The ladies in the
boxes who have already risen and put on their
wraps, stop to listen, and finally sit down again.)*

LE BRET
(To CYRANO)

Idiot!

A MEDDLER
(Hurries up to CYRANO.)
But what a scandal! Montfleury—
The great Montfleury! Did you know the Duc de Candale was
his patron? Who is yours?

CYRANO

No one.

THE MEDDLER

No one—no patron?

CYRANO

I said no.

THE MEDDLER

What, no great lord, to cover with his name—

CYRANO

(With visible annoyance)

No, I have told you twice. Must I repeat?
No sir, no patron—

(His hand on his sword)

But a patroness!

THE MEDDLER

And when do you leave Paris?

CYRANO

That's as may be.

THE MEDDLER

The Duc de Candale has a long arm.

CYRANO

Mine

Is longer,

(Drawing his sword)

by three feet of steel.

THE MEDDLER

Yes, yes,

But do you dream of daring—

CYRANO

I do dream

Of daring . . .

THE MEDDLER

But—

CYRANO

You may go now.

THE MEDDLER

But—

CYRANO

You may go—

Or tell me why are you staring at my nose!

THE MEDDLER

(In confusion)

No—I—

CYRANO

(Stepping up to him)

Does it astonish you?

THE MEDDLER

(Drawing back)

Your grace

Misunderstands my—

                    CYRANO
                         Is it long and soft
And dangling, like a trunk?

                    THE MEDDLER
        (Same business)

                                        I never said—

                    CYRANO
Or crooked, like an owl's beak?

                    THE MEDDLER

                                                    I—

                    CYRANO

                                        Perhaps

A pimple ornaments the end of it?

                    THE MEDDLER
No—

                    CYRANO
        Or a fly parading up and down?
What is this portent?

                    THE MEDDLER
                         Oh!—

                    CYRANO

                                    This phenomenon?

                    THE MEDDLER
But I have been careful not to look—

                    CYRANO

                                                And why

Not, if you please?

                    THE MEDDLER
                         Why—

                    CYRANO

                                        It disgusts you, then?

                    THE MEDDLER

My dear sir—

                    CYRANO
                         Does its color appear to you

Unwholesome?

                    THE MEDDLER
                    Oh, by no means!

                    CYRANO

                                            Or its form

Obscene?

                    THE MEDDLER
                    Not in the least—
                         28

Then why assume

This deprecating manner? Possibly
You find it just a trifle large?

THE MEDDLER

(Babbling)

Oh no!—

Small, very small, infinitesimal—

CYRANO

(Roars)

What?

How? You accuse me of absurdity?
Small—*my nose?* Why—

THE MEDDLER

(Breathless)

My God!—

CYRANO

Magnificent,

My nose! . . . You pug, you knob, you button-head,
Know that I glory in this nose of mine,
For a great nose indicates a great man—
Genial, courteous, intellectual,
Virile, courageous—as I am—and such
As you—poor wretch—will never dare to be
Even in imagination. For that face—
That blank, inglorious concavity
Which my right hand finds—

(He strikes him.)

THE MEDDLER

Ow!

CYRANO

—on top of you,

Is as devoid of pride, of poetry,
Of soul, of picturesqueness, of contour,
Of character, of NOSE in short—as that

*(Takes him by the shoulders and turns him around,
suiting the action to the word)*

Which at the end of that limp spine of yours
My left foot—

THE MEDDLER

(Escaping)

Help! The Guard!

CYRANO

Take notice, all

Who find this feature of my countenance

A theme for comedy! When the humorist
Is noble, then my custom is to show
Appreciation proper to his rank—
More heartfelt . . . and more pointed. . . .

DE GUICHE

*(Who has come down from the stage, surrounded
by the Marquis)*

Presently

This fellow will grow tiresome.

VALVERT

(Shrugs)

Oh, he blows

His trumpet!

DE GUICHE

Well—will no one interfere?

VALVERT

No one?

(Looks around)

Observe. I myself will proceed
To put him in his place.

*(He walks up to CYRANO, who has been watching
him, and stands there, looking him over with an
affected air.)*

Ah . . . your nose . . . hem! . . .

Your nose is . . . rather large!

CYRANO

(Gravely)

Rather.

VALVERT

(Simpering)

Oh well—

CYRANO

(Coolly)

Is that all?

VALVERT

(Turns away with a shrug)

Well, of course—

CYRANO

Ah, no, young sir!

You are too simple. Why, you might have said—
Oh, a great many things! Mon dieu, why waste
Your opportunity? For example, thus:—
AGGRESSIVE: I, sir, if that nose were mine,
I'd have it amputated—on the spot!
FRIENDLY: How do you drink with such a nose?

30

You ought to have a cup made specially.
DESCRIPTIVE: 'Tis a rock—a crag—a cape—
A cape? say rather, a peninsula!
INQUISITIVE: What is that receptacle—
A razor-case or a portfolio?
KINDLY: Ah, do you love the little birds
So much that when they come and sing to you,
You give them this to perch on? INSOLENT:
Sir, when you smoke, the neighbors must suppose
Your chimney is on fire. CAUTIOUS: Take care—
A weight like that might make you topheavy.
THOUGHTFUL: Somebody fetch my parasol—
Those delicate colors fade so in the sun!
PEDANTIC: Does not Aristophanes
Mention a mythologic monster called
Hippocampelephantocamelos?
Surely we have here the original!
FAMILIAR: Well, old torchlight! Hang your hat
Over that chandelier—it hurts my eyes.
ELOQUENT: When it blows, the typhoon howls,
And the clouds darken. DRAMATIC: When it bleeds—
The Red Sea! ENTERPRISING: What a sign
For some perfumer! LYRIC: Hark—the horn
Of Roland calls to summon Charlemagne!—
SIMPLE: When do they unveil the monument?
RESPECTFUL: Sir, I recognize in you
A man of parts, a man of prominence—
RUSTIC: Hey? What? Call that a nose? Na na—
I be no fool like what you think I be—
That there's a blue cucumber! MILITARY:
Point against cavalry! PRACTICAL: Why not
A lottery with this for the grand prize?
Or—parodying Faustus in the play—
"Was this the nose that launched a thousand ships
And burned the topless towers of Ilium?"
These, my dear sir, are things you might have said
Had you some tinge of letters, or of wit
To color your discourse. But wit,—not so,
You never had an atom—and of letters,
You need but three to write you down—an Ass.
Moreover,—if you had the invention, here
Before these folks to make a jest of me—
Be sure you would not then articulate
The twentieth part of half a syllable
Of the beginning! For I say these things

31

Lightly enough myself, about myself,
But I allow none else to utter them.

DE GUICHE
(Tries to lead away the amazed VALVERT.*)*

Vicomte—come.

VALVERT

(Choking)

            Oh— These arrogant grand airs!—
A clown who—look at him—not even gloves!
No ribbons—no lace—no buckles on his shoes—

CYRANO
I carry my adornments on my soul.
I do not dress up like a popinjay;
But inwardly, I keep my daintiness.
I do not bear with me, by any chance,
An insult not yet washed away—a conscience
Yellow with unpurged bile—an honor frayed
To rags, a set of scruples badly worn.
I go caparisoned in gems unseen,
Trailing white plumes of freedom, garlanded
With my good name—no figure of a man,
But a soul clothed in shining armor, hung
With deeds for decorations, twirling—thus—
A bristling wit, and swinging at my side
Courage, and on the stones of this old town
Making the sharp truth ring, like golden spurs!

VALVERT

But—

CYRANO
      But I have no gloves! A pity too!
I had one—the last one of an old pair—
And lost that. Very careless of me. Some
Gentleman offered me an impertinence.
I left it—in his face.

VALVERT

               Dolt, bumpkin, fool,
Insolent puppy, jobbernowl!

CYRANO
(Removes his hat and bows.)

                  Ah, yes?

And I—Cyrano-Savinien-Hercule
De Bergerac!

VALVERT

(Turns away.)

        Buffoon!

CYRANO
(Cries out as if suddenly taken with a cramp.)
Oh!

VALVERT
(Turns back.)
Well, what now?

CYRANO
(With grimaces of anguish)
I must do something to relieve these cramps—
This is what comes of lack of exercise—
Ah!—

VALVERT
What is all this?

CYRANO
My sword has gone to sleep?

VALVERT
(Draws)
So be it!

CYRANO
You shall die exquisitely.

VALVERT
(Contemptuously)
Poet!

CYRANO
Why yes, a poet, if you will;
So while we fence, I'll make you a Ballade
Extempore.

VALVERT
A Ballade?

CYRANO
Yes. You know
What that is?

VALVERT
I—

CYRANO
The Ballade, sir, is formed
Of three stanzas of eight lines each—

VALVERT
Oh, come!

CYRANO
And a refrain of four.

VALVERT
You—

CYRANO
I'll compose

One, while I fight with you; and at the end
Of the last line—thrust home!

VALVERT

Will you?

CYRANO

I will.

(Declaims)

"Ballade of the duel at the Hôtel de Bourgogne
Between de Bergerac and a Boeotian."

VALVERT

(Sneering)

What do you mean by that?

CYRANO

Oh, that? The title.

THE CROWD

(Excited)

Come on—

A circle—

Quiet—

Down in front!

(TABLEAU. *A ring of interested spectators in the
centre of the floor, the Marquis and the Officers
mingling with the citizens and common folk.
Pages swarming up on men's shoulders to see
better; the Ladies in the boxes standing and
leaning over. To the right,* DE GUICHE *and his
following; to the left,* LE BRET, CUIGY, RA-
GUENEAU, *and others of* CYRANO'S *friends.*)

CYRANO

(Closes his eyes for an instant.)

Stop . . . Let me choose my rimes. . . . Now!

Here we go—

*(He suits the action to the word, throughout the
following:)*

Lightly I toss my hat away,
  Languidly over my arm let fall
The cloak that covers my bright array—
  Then out swords, and to work withal!
  A Launcelot, in his Lady's hall . . .
  A Spartacus, at the Hippodrome! . . .
I dally awhile with you, dear jackal,
Then, as I end the refrain, thrust home!

(The swords cross—the fight is on.)

Where shall I skewer my peacock? . . . Nay,
  Better for you to have shunned this brawl!—

34

Here, in the heart, thro' your ribbons gay?
  —In the belly, under your silken shawl?
Hark, how the steel rings musical!
Mark how my point floats, light as the foam,
  Ready to drive you back to the wall,
Then, as I end the refrain, thrust home!

Ho, for a rime! . . . You are white as whey—
  You break, you cower, you cringe, you . . . crawl!
Tac!—and I parry your last essay:
  So may the turn of a hand forestall
  Life with its honey, death with its gall;
So may the turn of my fancy roam
  Free, for a time, till the rimes recall,
Then, as I end the refrain, thrust home!
          (He announces solemnly.)
Refrain:
  Prince! Pray God, that is Lord of all,
Pardon your soul, for your time has come!
  Beat—pass—fling you aslant, asprawl—
Then, as I end the refrain . . .
          *(He lunges; VALVERT staggers back and falls into
          the arms of his friends. CYRANO recovers, and
          salutes.)*

                              —Thrust home!
          *(Shouts. Applause from the boxes. Flowers and
          handkerchiefs come fluttering down. The Officers
          surround CYRANO and congratulate him. RA-
          GUENEAU dances for joy. LE BRET is unable to
          conceal his enthusiasm. The friends of VALVERT
          hold him up and help him away.)*

                    THE CROWD
          (In one long cry)

Ah-h!

                    A CAVALIER
          Superb!

                    A WOMAN
          Simply sweet!
                    RAGUENEAU

                              Magnelephant!

                    A MARQUIS

A novelty!

                    LE BRET
          Bah!

                    35

THE CROWD
(Thronging around CYRANO)
Compliments—regards—

Bravo!—

A WOMAN'S VOICE
Why, he's a hero!

A MUSKETEER
(Advances quickly to CYRANO, *with outstretched hands.)*
Monsieur, will you
Permit me?—It was altogether fine!
I think I may appreciate these things—
Moreover, I have been stamping for pure joy!
(He retires quickly.)

CYRANO
(To CUIGY)
What was that gentleman's name?

CUIGY
Oh . . . D'Artagnan.

LE BRET
(Takes CYRANO'S *arm.)*
Come here and tell me—

CYRANO
Let this crowd go first—
(To BELLEROSE)
May we stay?

BELLEROSE
(With great respect)
Certainly!
(Cries and cat-calls off stage.)

JODELET
(Comes down from the door where he has been looking out.)
Hark!— Montfleury—
They are hooting him.

BELLEROSE
(Solemnly)
"Sic transit gloria!"
(Changes his tone and shouts to the Porter and the Lamplighter.)
—Strike! . . . Close the house! . . . Leave the lights—
We rehearse
The new farce after dinner.
(JODELET and BELLEROSE go out after elaborately saluting CYRANO.)*

THE PORTER

(To Cyrano)

You do not dine?

CYRANO

I?— No!

(The Porter turns away.)

LE BRET

Why not?

CYRANO

(Haughtily)

Because—

(Changing his tone when he sees the Porter has gone.)

Because I have

No money.

LE BRET

(Gesture of tossing)

But—the purse of gold?

CYRANO

Farewell,

Paternal pension!

LE BRET

So you have, until

The first of next month—?

CYRANO

Nothing.

LE BRET

What a fool!—

CYRANO

But—what a gesture!

THE ORANGE GIRL

(Behind her little counter; coughs.)

Hem!

(Cyrano and Le Bret look around; she advances timidly.)

Pardon, monsieur . . .

A man ought never to go hungry . . .

(Indicating the sideboard)

See,

I have everything here . . .

(Eagerly)

Please !—

CYRANO

(Uncovers)

My dear child,

I cannot bend this Gascon pride of mine
To accept such a kindness— Yet, for fear
That I may give you pain if I refuse,
I will take . . .

(He goes to the sideboard and makes his selection.)

Oh, not very much! A grape . . .

(She gives him the bunch; he removes a single grape.)

One only! And a glass of water . . .

(She starts to pour wine into it; he stops her.)

Clear!

And . . . half a macaroon!

(He gravely returns the other half.)

LE BRET

Old idiot!

THE ORANGE GIRL

Please!— Nothing more?

CYRANO

Why yes— Your hand to kiss.

(He kisses the hand which she holds out, as he would the hand of a princess.)

THE ORANGE GIRL

Thank you, sir.

(She curtseys.)

Good-night.

(She goes out.)

CYRANO

Now, I am listening.

(Plants himself before the sideboard and arranges thereon—)

Dinner!—

(—the macaroon)

Drink!—

(—the glass of water)

Dessert!—

(—the grape.)

There—now I'll sit down.

(Seats himself.)

Lord, I was hungry! Abominably!

(Eating)

Well?

LE BRET

These fatheads with the bellicose grand airs
Will have you ruined if you listen to them;

Talk to a man of sense and hear how all
Your swagger impresses him.

CYRANO

(Finishes his macaroon)

Enormously.

LE BRET

The Cardinal—

CYRANO

(Beaming)

Was he there?

LE BRET

He must have thought you—

CYRANO

Original.

LE BRET

Well, but—

CYRANO

He is himself
A playwright. He will not be too displeased
That I have closed another author's play.

LE BRET

But look at all the enemies you have made!

CYRANO

(Begins on the grape.)

How many—do you think?

LE BRET

Just forty-eight

Without the women.

CYRANO

Count them.

LE BRET

Montfleury,

Baro, de Guiche, the Vicomte, the Old Man,
All the Academy—

CYRANO

Enough! You make me

Happy!

LE BRET

But where is all this leading you?
What is your plan?

CYRANO

I have been wandering—
Wasting my force upon too many plans.
Now I have chosen one.

LE BRET

What one?

CYRANO

The simplest—

To make myself in all things admirable!

LE BRET

Hmph!— Well, then, the real reason why you hate
Montfleury—Come, the truth, now!

CYRANO

(Rises)

That Silenus,

Who cannot hold his belly in his arms,
Still dreams of being sweetly dangerous
Among the women—sighs and languishes,
Making sheeps' eyes out of his great frog's face—
I hate him ever since one day he dared
Smile upon—

Oh, my friend, I seemed to see
Over some flower a great snail crawling!

LE BRET

(Amazed)

How,

What? Is it possible?—

CYRANO

(With a bitter smile)

For me to love? . . .

(Changing his tone; seriously)

I love.

LE BRET

May I know? You have never said—

CYRANO

Whom I love? Think a moment. Think of me—
Me, whom the plainest woman would despise—
Me, with this nose of mine that marches on
Before me by a quarter of an hour!
Whom should I love? Why—of course—it must be
The woman in the world most beautiful.

LE BRET

Most beautiful?

CYRANO

In all this world—most sweet;
Also most wise; most witty; and most fair!

LE BRET

Who and what is this woman?

Dangerous

Mortally, without meaning; exquisite
Without imagining. Nature's own snare
To allure manhood. A white rose wherein
Love lies in ambush for his natural prey.
Who knows her smile has known a perfect thing.
She creates grace in her own image, brings
Heaven to earth in one movement of her hand—
Nor thou, O Venus! balancing thy shell
Over the Mediterranean blue, nor thou,
Diana! marching through broad, blossoming woods,
Art so divine as when she mounts her chair,
And goes abroad through Paris!

LE BRET

Oh, well—of course,

That makes everything clear!

CYRANO

Transparently.

LE BRET

Madeleine Robin—your cousin?

CYRANO

Yes; Roxane.

LE BRET

And why not? If you love her, tell her so!
You have covered yourself with glory in her eyes
This very day.

CYRANO

My old friend—look at me,

And tell me how much hope remains for me
With this protuberance! Oh I have no more
Illusions! Now and then—bah! I may grow
Tender, walking alone in the blue cool
Of evening, through some garden fresh with flowers
After the benediction of the rain;
My poor big devil of a nose inhales
April . . . and so I follow with my eyes
Where some boy, with a girl upon his arm,
Passes a patch of silver . . . and I feel
Somehow, I wish I had a woman too,
Walking with little steps under the moon,
And holding my arm so, and smiling. Then
I dream—and I forget. . . .

And then I see

The shadow of my profile on the wall!

LE BRET

My friend ! . . .

CYRANO

My friend, I have my bitter days,
Knowing myself so ugly, so alone.
Sometimes—

LE BRET

You weep?

CYRANO

(Quickly)

Oh, not that ever ! No,
That would be too grotesque—tears trickling down
All the long way along this nose of mine?
I will not so profane the dignity
Of sorrow. Never any tears for me !
Why, there is nothing more sublime than tears,
Nothing !—Shall I make them ridiculous
In my poor person?

LE BRET

Love's no more than chance !

CYRANO

(Shakes his head.)

No. I love Cleopatra; do I appear
Cæsar? I adore Beatrice; have I
The look of Dante?

LE BRET

But your wit—your courage—
Why, that poor child who offered you just now
Your dinner ! She—you saw with your own eyes,
Her eyes did not avoid you.

CYRANO

(Thoughtful.)

That is true . . .

LE BRET

Well then ! Roxane herself, watching your duel,
Paler than—

CYRANO

Pale?—

LE BRET

Her lips parted, her hand
Thus, at her breast— I saw it ! Speak to her
Speak, man !

CYRANO

Through my nose? She might laugh at me;
That is the one thing in this world I fear !

(Followed by the Duenna, approaches CYRANO
respectfully.)

A lady asking for Monsieur.

CYRANO

Mon dieu ...

Her Duenna!—

THE DUENNA
(A sweeping curtsey)
Monsieur ...

A message for you:
From our good cousin we desire to know
When and where we may see him privately.

CYRANO
(Amazed)

To see me?

THE DUENNA
(An elaborate reverence)
To see you. We have certain things
To tell you.

CYRANO

Certain—

THE DUENNA
Things.

CYRANO
(Trembling)

Mon dieu! ...

THE DUENNA

We go

To-morrow, at the first flush of the dawn,
To hear Mass at St. Roch. Then afterwards,
Where can we meet and talk a little?

CYRANO
(Catching LE BRET'S *arm.)*

Where?—

I— Ah, mon dieu! ... mon dieu! ...

THE DUENNA

Well?

CYRANO

I am thinking ...

THE DUENNA

And you think?

CYRANO
I ... The shop of Ragueneau ...
Ragueneau—pastrycook ...

43

Who dwells?—

CYRANO

Mon dieu! . . .

Oh, yes . . . Ah, mon dieu! . . . Rue St.-Honoré.

THE DUENNA

We are agreed. Remember—seven o'clock.
(Reverence)

Until then—

CYRANO

I'll be there.
(The Duenna goes out.)

CYRANO

(Falls into the arms of LE BRET.*)*

Me . . . to see me! . . .

LE BRET

You are not quite so gloomy.

CYRANO

After all,

She knows that I exist—no matter why!

LE BRET

So now, you are going to be happy.

CYRANO

Now! . . .

(Beside himself)

I—I am going to be a storm—a flame—
I need to fight whole armies all alone;
I have ten hearts; I have a hundred arms; I feel
Too strong to war with mortals—
(He shouts at the top of his voice.)

BRING ME GIANTS!

*(A moment since, the shadows of the comedians
have been visible moving and posturing upon the
stage. The violins have taken their places.)*

A VOICE

(From the stage)

Hey—pst—less noise! We are rehearsing here!

CYRANO

(Laughs)

We are going.
*(He turns up stage. Through the street door enter
CUIGY, BRISSAILLE, and a number of officers,
supporting LIGNIÈRE, who is now thoroughly
drunk.)*

CUIGY

Cyrano!

CYRANO

What is it?

CUIGY

Here—

Here's your stray lamb!

CYRANO

(Recognizes LIGNIÈRE.)

Lignière—What's wrong with him?

CUIGY

He wants you.

BRISSAILLE

He's afraid to go home.

CYRANO

Why?

LIGNIÈRE

*(Showing a crumpled scrap of paper and speaking
with the elaborate logic of profound intoxication.)*

This letter—hundred against one—that's me—
I'm the one—all because of little song—
Good song— Hundred men, waiting, understand?
Porte de Nesle—way home— Might be dangerous—
Would you permit me spend the night with you?

CYRANO

A hundred—is that all? You are going home!

LIGNIÈRE

(Astonished)

Why—

CYRANO

*(In a voice of thunder, indicating the lighted lan-
tern which the Porter holds up curiously as he
regards the scene.)*

Take that lantern!

*(*LIGNIÈRE *precipitately seizes the lantern.)*

Forward march! I say

I'll be the man to-night that sees you home.

(To the officers)

You others follow—I want an audience!

CUIGY

A hundred against one—

CYRANO

Those are the odds

To-night!

45

(The Comedians in their costumes are descending from the stage and joining the group.)

LE BRET

But why help this—

CYRANO

There goes Le Bret

Growling!

LE BRET

—This drunkard here?

CYRANO

(His hand on LE BRET's *shoulder.)*

Because this drunkard—
This tun of sack, this butt of Burgundy—
Once in his life has done one lovely thing:
After the Mass, according to the form,
He saw, one day, the lady of his heart
Take holy water for a blessing. So
This one, who shudders at a drop of rain,
This fellow here—runs headlong to the font
Bends down and drinks it dry!

A SOUBRETTE

I say that was

A pretty thought!

CYRANO

Ah, was it not?

THE SOUBRETTE

(To the others)

But why

Against one poor poet, a hundred men?

CYRANO

March!

(To the officers)

And you gentlemen, remember now,
No rescue— Let me fight alone.

A COMEDIENNE

(Jumps down from the stage.)

Come on!

I'm going to watch—

CYRANO

Come along!

ANOTHER COMEDIENNE

(Jumps down, speaks to a Comedian costumed as an old man.)

You, Cassandre?

Come all of you—the Doctor, Isabelle,
Léandre—the whole company—a swarm
Of murmuring, golden bees—we'll parody
Italian farce and Tragedy-of-Blood;
Ribbons for banners, masks for blazonry,
And tambourines to be our rolling drums!

ALL THE WOMEN
(Jumping for joy.)

Bravo!—My hood— My cloak— Hurry!

JODELET
(Mock heroic)

Lead on!—

CYRANO
(To the violins)

You violins—play us an overture—
*(The violins join the procession which is forming.
The lighted candles are snatched from the stage
and distributed; it becomes a torchlight procession.)*

Bravo!—Officers— Ladies in costume—
And twenty paces in advance . . .
(He takes his station as he speaks.)

Myself,

Alone, with glory fluttering over me,
Alone as Lucifer at war with heaven!
Remember—no one lifts a hand to help—
Ready there? One . . . two . . . three! Porter, the doors! . . .
*(The Porter flings wide the great doors. We see in
the dim moonlight a corner of old Paris, purple
and picturesque.)*

Look—Paris dreams—nocturnal, nebulous,
Under blue moonbeams hung from wall to wall—
Nature's own setting for the scene we play!—
Yonder, behind her veil of mist, the Seine,
Like a mysterious and magic mirror
Trembles—
And you shall see what you shall see!

ALL
To the Porte de Nesle!

CYRANO
(Erect upon the threshold)

To the Porte de Nesle!
(He turns back for a moment to the Soubrette)

Did you not ask, my dear, why against one

Singer they send a hundred swords?
          (Quietly, drawing his own sword)

                                        Because
They know this one man for a friend of mine!
          (He goes out. The procession follows: LIGNIÈRE
          *zigzagging at its head, then the Comediennes on
          the arms of the Officers, then the Comedians,
          leaping and dancing as they go. It vanishes into
          the night to the music of the violins, illuminated
          by the flickering glimmer of the candles.)*
                    (Curtain)

THE SECOND ACT

·

THE SHOP OF RAGUENEAU, *Baker and Pastrycook: a spacious affair at the corner of the Rue St.-Honoré and the Rue de l'Arbre Sec. The street, seen vaguely through the glass panes in the door at the back, is gray in the first light of dawn.*

In the foreground, at the Left, a Counter is surmounted by a Canopy of wrought iron from which are hanging ducks, geese, and white peacocks. Great crockery jars hold bouquets of common flowers, yellow sunflowers in particular. On the same side farther back, a huge fireplace; in front of it, between great andirons, of which each one supports a little saucepan, roast fowls revolve and weep into their dripping-pans. To the Right at the First Entrance, a door. Beyond it, Second Entrance, a staircase leads up to a little dining-room under the eaves, its interior visible through open shutters. A table is set there and a tiny Flemish candlestick is lighted; there one may retire to eat and drink in private. A wooden gallery, extending from the head of the stairway, seems to lead to other little dining-rooms.

In the centre of the shop, an iron ring hangs by a rope over a pulley so that it can be raised or lowered; adorned with game of various kinds hung from it by hooks, it has the appearance of a sort of gastronomic chandelier.

In the shadow under the staircase, ovens are glowing. The spits revolve; the copper pots and pans gleam ruddily. Pastries in pyramids. Hams hanging from the rafters. The morning baking is in progress: a bustle of tall cooks and timid scullions and scurrying apprentices; a blossoming of white caps adorned with cock's feathers or the wings of guinea fowl. On wicker trays or on great metal platters they bring in rows of pastries and fancy dishes of various kinds.

Tables are covered with trays of cakes and rolls; others with chairs placed about them are set for guests.

One little table in a corner disappears under a heap of

papers. At the CURTAIN RISE RAGUENEAU *is seated there. He is writing poetry.*

A PASTRYCOOK
(Brings in a dish.)

Fruits en gelée!

SECOND PASTRYCOOK
(Brings dish.)

Custard!

THIRD PASTRYCOOK
(Brings roast peacock ornamented with feathers.)

Peacock rôti!

FOURTH PASTRYCOOK
(Brings tray of cakes.)

Cakes and confections!

FIFTH PASTRYCOOK
(Brings earthen dish.)

Beef en casserole!

RAGUENEAU
(Raises his head; returns to mere earth.)

Over the coppers of my kitchen flows
The frosted-silver dawn. Silence awhile
The god who sings within thee, Ragueneau!
Lay down the lute—the oven calls for thee!
(Rises; goes to one of the cooks.)
Here's a hiatus in your sauce; fill up
The measure.

THE COOK
How much?

RAGUENEAU
(Measures on his finger.)

One more dactyl.

THE COOK

Huh? . . .

FIRST PASTRYCOOK

Rolls!

SECOND PASTRYCOOK
Roulades!

RAGUENEAU
(Before the fireplace)

Veil, O Muse, thy virgin eyes
From the lewd gleam of these terrestrial fires!
(To First Pastrycook)
Your rolls lack balance. Here's the proper form—
An equal hemistich on either side,
And the caesura in between.

50

(To another, pointing out an unfinished pie)
                                        Your house
Of crust should have a roof upon it.
            *(To another, who is seated on the hearth, placing
                poultry on a spit)*
                                        And you—
Along the interminable spit, arrange
The modest pullet and the lordly Turk
Alternately, my son—as great Malherbe
Alternates male and female rimes. Remember,
A couplet, or a roast, should be well turned.

AN APPRENTICE
        (Advances with a dish covered by a napkin.)
Master, I thought of you when I designed
This, hoping it might please you.

RAGUENEAU
                                        Ah! A lyre—

THE APPRENTICE
In puff-paste—

RAGUENEAU
            And the jewels—candied fruit!

THE APPRENTICE
And the strings, barley-sugar!

RAGUENEAU
        (Gives him money.)
                                        Go and drink
My health.
        (LISE enters.)
                        St!—My wife— Circulate, and hide
That money!
            (Shows the lyre to LISE, with a languid air.)
                        Graceful—yes?

LISE
                                        Ridiculous!
(She places on the counter a pile of paper bags.)

RAGUENEAU
Paper bags? Thank you . . .
        (He looks at them.)
                                        Ciel! My manuscripts!
The sacred verses of my poets—rent
Asunder, limb from limb—butchered to make
Base packages of pastry! Ah, you are one
Of those insane Bacchantes who destroyed
Orpheus!

LISE

Your dirty poets left them here
To pay for eating half our stock-in-trade:
We ought to make some profit out of them!

RAGUENEAU

Ant! Would you blame the locust for his song?

LISE

I blame the locust for his appetite!
There used to be a time—before you had
Your hungry friends—you never called me Ants—
No, nor Bacchantes!

RAGUENEAU

What a way to use

Poetry!

LISE

Well, what is the use of it?

RAGUENEAU

But, my dear girl, what would you do with prose?
(Two children enter.)
Well, dears?

A CHILD

Three little patties.

RAGUENEAU

(Serves them.)

There we are!

All hot and brown.

THE CHILD

Would you mind wrapping them?

RAGUENEAU

One of my paper bags! . . .

Oh, certainly.
*(Reads from the bag, as he is about to wrap the
patties in it.)*
"Ulysses, when he left Penelope"—
Not that one!
(Takes another bag; reads.)
"Phoebus, golden-crowned"—

Not that one.

LISE

Well? They are waiting!

RAGUENEAU

Very well, very well!—

The Sonnet to Phyllis . . .

Yet—it does seem hard . . .

Made up your mind—at last! Mph!—Jack-o'-Dreams!

RAGUENEAU

(As her back is turned, calls back the children, who are already at the door.)

Pst!—Children— Give me back the bag. Instead
Of three patties, you shall have six of them!

(Makes the exchange. The children go out. He reads from the bag, as he smooths it out tenderly.)

"Phyllis"—

A spot of butter on her name!—

"Phyllis"—

CYRANO

(Enters hurriedly.)

What is the time?

RAGUENEAU

Six o'clock.

CYRANO

One
Hour more . . .

RAGUENEAU

Felicitations!

CYRANO

And for what?

RAGUENEAU

Your victory! I saw it all—

CYRANO

Which one?

RAGUENEAU

At the Hôtel de Bourgogne.

CYRANO

Oh—the duel!

RAGUENEAU

The duel in Rime!

LISE

He talks of nothing else.

CYRANO

Nonsense!

RAGUENEAU

(Fencing and foining with a spit, which he snatches up from the hearth.)

"Then, as I end the refrain, thrust home!"
"Then, as I end the refrain"—

Gods! What a line!

"Then, as I end"—

CYRANO
What time now, Ragueneau?

RAGUENEAU

(Petrified at the full extent of a lunge, while he looks at the clock.)

Five after six—

(Recovers)

"—thrust home!"

A Ballade, too!

LISE

(To CYRANO, *who in passing has mechanically shaken hands with her)*

Your hand—what have you done?

CYRANO

Oh, my hand?—Nothing.

RAGUENEAU

What danger now—

CYRANO
No danger.

LISE

I believe

He is lying.

CYRANO
Why? Was I looking down my nose?

That must have been a devil of a lie!

(Changing his tone; to RAGUENEAU)

I expect someone. Leave us here alone,
When the times comes.

RAGUENEAU

How can I? In a moment,

My poets will be here.

LISE

To break their . . . fast!

CYRANO

Take them away, then, when I give the sign.
—What time?

RAGUENEAU
Ten minutes after.

CYRANO

Have you a pen?

RAGUENEAU

(Offers him a pen.)

An eagle's feather!

A MUSKETEER
(Enters, and speaks to LISE *in a stentorian voice.)*
Greeting!

CYRANO

(To RAGUENEAU*)*

Who is this?

RAGUENEAU

My wife's friend. A terrific warrior,
So he says.

CYRANO

Ah— I see.
(Takes up the pen; waves RAGUENEAU *away.)*
Only to write—
To fold— To give it to her—and to go . . .
(Throws down the pen.)
Coward! And yet—the Devil take my soul
If I dare speak one word to her . . .
(To RAGUENEAU*)*

What time now?

RAGUENEAU

A quarter after six.

CYRANO

(Striking his breast)

—One little word
Of all the many thousand I have here!
Whereas in writing . . .
(Takes up the pen.)
Come, I'll write to her
That letter I have written on my heart,
Torn up, and written over many times—
So many times . . . that all I have to do
Is to remember, and to write it down.
*(He writes. Through the glass of the door appear
vague and hesitating shadows. The Poets enter,
clothed in rusty black and spotted with mud.)*

LISE

(To RAGUENEAU*)*
Here come your scarecrows!

FIRST POET

Comrade!

SECOND POET

(Takes both RAGUENEAU's *hands.)*
My dear brother!

THIRD POET

(Sniffing)

55

O Lord of Roasts, how sweet thy dwellings are!

FOURTH POET

Phoebus Apollo of the Silver Spoon!

FIFTH POET

Cupid of Cookery!

RAGUENEAU
(Surrounded, embraced, beaten on the back.)

These geniuses,
They put one at one's ease!

FIRST POET

We were delayed
By the crowd at the Porte de Nesle.

SECOND POET

Dead men
All scarred and gory, scattered on the stones,
Villainous-looking scoundrels—eight of them.

CYRANO
(Looks up an instant.)
Eight? I thought only seven—

RAGUENEAU

Do you know
The hero of this hecatomb?

CYRANO

I? . . . No.

LISE
(To the Musketeer)
Do you?

THE MUSKETEER
Hmm—perhaps!

FIRST POET

They say one man alone
Put to flight all this crowd.

SECOND POET

Everywhere lay
Swords, daggers, pikes, bludgeons—

CYRANO
(Writing)

"Your eyes . . ."

THIRD POET

As far
As the Quai des Orfevres, hats and cloaks—

FIRST POET

Why, that man must have been the devil!

CYRANO

"Your lips . . ."

Some savage monster might have done this thing!
"Looking upon you, I grow faint with fear . . ."
What have you written lately, Ragueneau?
"Your Friend— Who loves you . . ."
So. No signature;

I'll give it to her myself.
A Recipe

In Rime.

Read us your rimes!

Here's a brioche

Cocking its hat at me.
(He bites off the top of it.)
Look how those buns

Follow the hungry poet with their eyes—
Those almond eyes!

We are listening—
See this cream-puff—

Fat little baby, drooling while it smiles!
(Nibbling at the pastry lyre.)
For the first time, the lyre is my support.
(Coughs, adjusts his cap, strikes an attitude.)
A Recipe in Rime—

(Gives FIRST POET *a dig with his elbow.)*
Your breakfast?

Dinner!

(Declaims)
A Recipe for Making Almond Tarts

Beat your eggs, the yolk and white,
Very light;

Mingle with their creamy fluff
   Drops of lime-juice, cool and green;
      Then pour in
Milk of Almonds, just enough.

Dainty patty-pans, embraced
      In puff-paste—
Have these ready within reach;
   With your thumb and finger, pinch
      Half an inch
Up around the edge of each—

Into these, a score or more,
      Slowly pour
All your store of custard; so
   Take them, bake them golden-brown—
      Now sit down! . . .
Almond tartlets, Ragueneau!

THE POETS

Delicious! Melting!

A POET

(Chokes)

      Humph!
CYRANO

(To RAGUENEAU)

               Do you not see
Those fellows fattening themselves?—
RAGUENEAU

                  I know.

I would not look—it might embarrass them—
You see, I love a friendly audience.
Besides—another vanity—I am pleased
When they enjoy my cooking.
CYRANO
(Slaps him on the back.)

               Be off with you!—
    *(*RAGUENEAU *goes upstage.)*
Good little soul!
    (Calls to LISE.)

        Madame!—
    (She leaves the Musketeer and comes down to him.)

              This musketeer—
He is making love to you?
LISE

(Haughtily)

                                        If any man
Offends my virtue—all I have to do
Is look at him—once!

>   CYRANO
>   *(Looks at her gravely; she drops her eyes.)*
                                        I do not find
Those eyes of yours unconquerable.

>   LISE
>   *(Panting)*
                                        —Ah!

>   CYRANO
>   *(Raising his voice a little.)*
Now listen— I am fond of Ragueneau;
I allow no one—do you understand?—
To . . . take his name in vain!

>   LISE
                                        You think—

>   CYRANO
>   *(Ironic emphasis)*
                                        I think
I interrupt you.

>   *(He salutes the Musketeer, who has heard without
>   daring to resent the warning. LISE goes to the
>   Musketeer as he returns CYRANO's salute.)*

>   LISE
                        You—you swallow that?—
You ought to have pulled his nose!

>   THE MUSKETEER
>   His nose?—His nose! . . .
>   *(He goes out hurriedly. ROXANE and the Duenna
>   appear outside the door.)*

>   CYRANO
>   *(Nods to RAGUENEAU.)*
Pst!—

>   RAGUENEAU
>   *(To the Poets)*
Come inside—

>   CYRANO
>   *(Impatient)*
                        Pst! . . . Pst! . . .

>   RAGUENEAU
>   We shall be more
Comfortable . . .

>   *(He leads the Poets into inner room.)*

FIRST POET

The cakes!

SECOND POET

Bring them along!   *(They go out.)*

CYRANO

If I can see the faintest spark of hope,
Then—

(Throws door open—bows.)

Welcome!

*(ROXANE enters, followed by the Duenna, whom
CYRANO detains.)*

Pardon me—one word—

THE DUENNA

Take two.

CYRANO

Have you a good digestion?

THE DUENNA

Wonderful!

CYRANO

Good. Here are two sonnets, by Benserade—

THE DUENNA

Euh?

CYRANO

Which I fill for you with éclairs.

THE DUENNA

Ooo!

CYRANO

Do you like cream-puffs?

THE DUENNA

Only with whipped cream.

CYRANO

Here are three . . . six—embosomed in a poem
By Saint-Amant. This ode of Chapelin
Looks deep enough to hold—a jelly roll.
—Do you love Nature?

THE DUENNA

Mad about it.

CYRANO

Then

Go out and eat these in the street. Do not
Return—

THE DUENNA

Oh, but—

CYRANO

Until you finish them.

(Down to ROXANE*)*
Blessed above all others be the hour
When you remembered to remember me,
And came to tell me . . . what?

ROXANE
(Takes off her mask.)

First let me thank you
Because . . . That man . . . that creature, whom your sword
Made sport of yesterday— His patron, one—

CYRANO
De Guiche?—

ROXANE
—who thinks himself in love with me
Would have forced that man upon me for—
a husband—

CYRANO
I understand—so much the better then!
I fought, not for my nose, but your bright eyes.

ROXANE
And then, to tell you—but before I can
Tell you— Are you, I wonder, still the same
Big brother—almost—that you used to be
When we were children, playing by the pond
In the old garden down there—

CYRANO
I remember—
Every summer you came to Bergerac! . . .

ROXANE
You used to make swords out of bulrushes—

CYRANO
Your dandelion-dolls with golden hair—

ROXANE
And those green plums—

CYRANO
And those black mulberries—

ROXANE
In those days, you did everything I wished!

CYRANO
Roxane, in short skirts, was called Madeleine.

ROXANE
Was I pretty?

CYRANO
Oh—not too plain!

ROXANE
Sometimes

61

When you had hurt your hand you used to come
Running to me—and I would be your mother,
And say— Oh, in a very grown-up voice:
                    (She takes his hand.)
"Now, what have you been doing to yourself?
Let me see—"
                    (She sees the hand—starts.)
                Oh!—
                            Wait— I said, "Let me see!"
Still—at your age! How did you do that?

CYRANO

                                            Playing
With the big boys, down by the Porte de Nesle.

ROXANE

                    *(Sits at a table and wets her handkerchief in a
                        glass of water.)*
Come here to me.

CYRANO

                —Such a wise little mother!

ROXANE

And tell me, while I wash this blood away,
How many you—played with?

CYRANO

                                Oh, about a hundred.

ROXANE

Tell me.

CYRANO

                No. Let me go. Tell me what you
Were going to tell me—if you dared?

ROXANE

                    (Still holding his hand)

                                            I think
I do dare—now. It seems like long ago
When I could tell you things. Yes—I dare . . .
    Listen:
I . . . love someone.

CYRANO

                Ah! . . .

ROXANE

                            Someone who does not know.

Ah! . . .

ROXANE

        At least—not yet.

CYRANO

                        Ah! . . .

62

ROXANE

But he will know

Some day.

CYRANO

Ah! . . .

ROXANE

A big boy who loves me too,

And is afraid of me, and keeps away,
And never says one word.

CYRANO

Ah! . . .

ROXANE

Let me have

Your hand a moment—why how hot it is!—
I know. I see him trying . . .

CYRANO

Ah! . . .

ROXANE

There now!

Is that better?—
*(She finishes bandaging the hand with her handker-
chief.)*
Besides—only to think—
(This is a secret.) He is a soldier too,
In your own regiment—

CYRANO

Ah! . . .

ROXANE

Yes, in the Guards,

Your company too.

CYRANO

Ah! . . .

ROXANE

And such a man!—

He is proud—noble—young—brave—beautiful—

CYRANO

(Turns pale; rises.)

Beautiful!—

ROXANE

What's the matter?

CYRANO

(Smiling)

Nothing—this—

My sore hand!

63

ROXANE

Well, I love him. That is all.
Oh—and I never saw him anywhere
Except the *Comedie*.

CYRANO

You have never spoken?—

ROXANE

Only our eyes . . .

CYRANO

Why, then— How do you know?—

ROXANE

People talk about people; and I hear
Things . . . and I know.

CYRANO

You say he is in the Guards:

His name?

ROXANE

Baron Christian de Neuvillette.

CYRANO

He is not in the Guards.

ROXANE

Yes. Since this morning.
Captain Carbon de Castel-Jaloux.

CYRANO

So soon! . . .

So soon we lose our hearts!—

But, my dear child,—

THE DUENNA

(Opens the door.)
I have eaten the cakes, Monsieur de Bergerac!

CYRANO

Good! Now go out and read the poetry!
(The Duenna disappears.)
—But, my dear child! You, who love only words,
Wit, the grand manner— Why, for all you know,
The man may be a savage, or a fool.

ROXANE

His curls are like a hero from D'Urfé.

CYRANO

His mind may be as curly as his hair.

ROXANE

Not with such eyes. I read his soul in them.

CYRANO

Yes, all our souls are written in our eyes!
But—if he be a bungler?

64

ROXANE

Then I shall die—

There!

CYRANO

(After a pause)

And you brought me here to tell me this?
I do not yet quite understand, Madame,
The reason for your confidence.

ROXANE

They say

That in your company— It frightens me—
You are all Gascons . . .

CYRANO

And we pick a quarrel

With any flat-foot who intrudes himself.
Whose blood is not pure Gascon like our own?
Is this what you have heard?

ROXANE

I am so afraid

For him!

CYRANO

(Between his teeth)

Not without reason!—

ROXANE

And I thought

You . . . You were so brave, so invincible
Yesterday, against all those brutes!—If you,
Whom they all fear—

CYRANO

Oh well— I will defend

Your little Baron.

ROXANE

Will you? Just for me?

Because I have always been—your friend!

CYRANO

Of course . . .

ROXANE

Will you be *his* friend?

CYRANO

I will be his friend.

ROXANE

And never let him fight a duel?

CYRANO

No—never.

Oh, but you are a darling!—I must go—
You never told me about last night— Why,
You must have been a hero! Have him write
And tell me all about it—will you?

CYRANO

Of course . . .

ROXANE

(Kisses her hand.)
I always did love you!—A hundred men
Against one— Well. . . . Adieu. We are great friends,
Are we not?

CYRANO

Of course . . .

ROXANE

He *must* write to me—
A hundred— You shall tell me the whole story
Some day, when I have time. A hundred men—
What courage—

CYRANO

(Salutes as she goes out.)
Oh . . . I have done better since!
*(The door closes after her. CYRANO remains motion-
less, his eyes on the ground. Pause. The other
door opens; RAGUENEAU puts in his head.)*

RAGUENEAU

May I come in?

CYRANO

(Without moving)
Yes . . .
*(RAGUENEAU and his friends re-enter. At the same
time, CARBON DE CASTEL-JALOUX appears at the
street door in uniform as Captain of the Guards;
recognizes CYRANO with a sweeping gesture.)*

CARBON

Here he is!—Our hero!

CYRANO

(Raises his head and salutes.)
Our Captain!

CARBON

We know! All our company
Are here—

CYRANO

(Recoils)
No—

66

CARBON

Come! They are waiting for you.

CYRANO

No!

CARBON

(Tries to lead him out.)

Only across the street— Come!

CYRANO

Please—

CARBON

(Goes to the door and shouts in a voice of thunder.)

Our champion

Refuses! He is not feeling well to-day!

A VOICE OUTSIDE

Ah! Sandious!

(Noise outside of swords and trampling feet approaching.)

CARBON

Here they come now!

THE CADETS

(Entering the shop)

Mille dious!—

Mordious!—Capdedious!—Pocapdedious!

RAGUENEAU

(In astonishment)

Gentlemen—

You are all Gascons?

THE CADETS

All!

FIRST CADET

(To CYRANO*)*

Bravo!

CYRANO

Baron!

ANOTHER CADET

(Takes both his hands.)

Vivat!

CYRANO

Baron!

THIRD CADET

Come to my arms!

CYRANO

Baron!

OTHERS

To mine!—To mine!—

CYRANO

Baron . . . Baron . . . Have mercy—

RAGUENEAU

You are all Barons too?

THE CADETS

Are we?

RAGUENEAU

Are they? . . .

FIRST CADET

Our coronets would star the midnight sky!

LE BRET

(Enters: Hurries to CYRANO.*)*

The whole town's looking for you! Raving mad—
A triumph! Those who saw the fight—

CYRANO

I hope

You have not told them where I—

LE BRET

(Rubbing his hands)

Certainly

I told them!

CITIZEN

(Enters, followed by a group.)

Listen! Shut the door!—Here comes

All Paris!

*(The street outside fills with a shouting crowd.
Chairs and carriages stop at the door.)*

LE BRET

(Aside to CYRANO, *smiling)*

And Roxane?

CYRANO

(Quickly)

Hush!

THE CROWD OUTSIDE

Cyrano!

*(A mob bursts into the shop. Shouts, acclamations,
general disturbance.)*

RAGUENEAU

(Standing on a table.)

My shop invaded— They'll break everything—
Glorious!

SEVERAL MEN

(Crowding about CYRANO*)*

My friend! . . . My friend! . . .

68

CYRANO

                                        Why, yesterday
I did not have so many friends!
                    LE BRET

                                Success
At last!
                        A MARQUIS
            (Runs to CYRANO, with outstretched hands)
            My dear—really!—
                        CYRANO
        (Coldly)

                                So? And how long
Have I been dear to you?
                        ANOTHER MARQUIS
                            One moment—pray!
I have two ladies in my carriage here;
Let me present you—
                        CYRANO

                            Certainly! And first,
Who will present you, sir,—to me?
                        LE BRET
            (Astounded)

                                        Why, what
The devil?—
                        CYRANO
            Hush!
                    A MAN OF LETTERS
            (With a portfolio)

                                May I have the details?...
                        CYRANO
You may not.
                        LE BRET
            (Plucking CYRANO's sleeve)
                            Theophraste Renaudot!—Editor
Of the *Gazette*—your reputation!...
                        CYRANO

                                            No!

                        A POET
            (Advances)
Monsieur—
                        CYRANO
            Well?
                        THE POET
                            Your full name? I will compose
A pentacrostic—

                            69

Monsieur—

CYRANO

That will do!

(Movement. The crowd arranges itself. DE GUICHE
appears, escorted by CUIGY, BRISSAILLE, and the
other officers who were with CYRANO at the close
of the First Act.)

CUIGY

(Goes to CYRANO.)

Monsieur de Guiche!—

(Murmur. Everyone moves.)

A message from the Marshal

De Gassion—

DE GUICHE

(Saluting CYRANO)

Who wishes to express

Through me his admiration. He has heard
Of your affair—

THE CROWD

Bravo!

CYRANO

(Bowing)

The Marshal speaks

As an authority.

DE GUICHE

He said just now

The story would have been incredible
Were it not for the witness—

CUIGY

Of our eyes!

LE BRET

(Aside to CYRANO)

What is it?

CYRANO

Hush!—

LE BRET

Something is wrong with you;

Are you in pain?

CYRANO

(Recovering himself)

In pain? Before this crowd?

(His moustache bristles. He throws out his chest.)

I? In pain? You shall see!

70

DE GUICHE
(To whom CUIGY *has been whispering.)*

Your name is known

Already as a soldier. You are one
Of those wild Gascons, are you not?

CYRANO

The Guards,

Yes. A Cadet.

A CADET
(In a voice of thunder)·

One of ourselves!

DE GUICHE

Ah! So—

Then all these gentlemen with the haughty air,
These are the famous—

CARBON

Cyrano!

CYRANO

Captain?

CARBON

Our troop being all present, be so kind
As to present them to the Comte de Guiche!

CYRANO
(With a gesture presenting the Cadets to DE
GUICHE, *declaims:)*

The Cadets of Gascoyne—the defenders
    of Carbon de Castel-Jaloux:
Free fighters, free lovers, free spenders—
The Cadets of Gascoyne—the defenders
Of old homes, old names, and old splendors—
    A proud and a pestilent crew!
The Cadets of Gascoyne, the defenders
    Of Carbon de Castel-Jaloux.

Hawk-eyed, they stare down all contenders—
    The wolf bares his fangs as they do—
Make way there, you fat money-lenders!
(Hawk-eyed, they stare down all contenders)
Old boots that have been to the menders,
    Old cloaks that are worn through and through—
Hawk-eyed, they stare down all contenders—
    The wolf bares his fangs as they do!

Skull-breakers they are, and sword-benders;
    Red blood is their favorite brew;

71

Hot haters and loyal befrienders,
Skull-breakers they are, and sword-benders.
Wherever a quarrel engenders,
   They're ready and waiting for you!
Skull-breakers they are, and sword-benders;
   Red blood is their favorite brew!

Behold them, our Gascon defenders
   Who win every woman they woo!
There's never a dame but surrenders—
Behold them, our Gascon defenders!
Young wives who are clever pretenders—
   Old husbands who house the cuckoo—
Behold them—our Gascon defenders
   Who win every woman they woo!

DE GUICHE
(Languidly, sitting in a chair)
Poets are fashionable nowadays
To have about one. Would you care to join
My following?

CYRANO
       No, sir. I do not follow.

DE GUICHE
Your duel yesterday amused my uncle
The Cardinal. I might help you there.

LE BRET
                Grand Dieu!

DE GUICHE
I suppose you have written a tragedy—
They all have.

LE BRET
(Aside to CYRANO)
       Now at last you'll have it played—
Your "Agrippine!"

DE GUICHE
       Why not? Take it to him.

CYRANO
(Tempted)
Really—

DE GUICHE
     He is himself a dramatist;
Let him rewrite a few lines here and there,
And he'll approve the rest.

CYRANO
(His face falls again.)
Impossible.
My blood curdles to think of altering
One comma.

DE GUICHE
Ah, but when he likes a thing
He pays well.

CYRANO
Yes—but not so well as I—
When I have made a line that sings itself
So that I love the sound of it—I pay
Myself a hundred times.

DE GUICHE
You are proud, my friend.

CYRANO
You have observed that?

A CADET
*(Enters with a drawn sword, along the whole blade
of which is transfixed a collection of disreputable
hats, their plumes draggled, their crowns cut and
torn.)*
Cyrano! See here—
Look what we found this morning in the street—
The plumes dropped in their flight by those fine birds
Who showed the white feather!

CARBON
Spoils of the hunt—
Well mounted!

THE CROWD
Ha-ha-ha!

CUIGY
Whoever hired
Those rascals, he must be an angry man
To-day!

BRISSAILLE
Who was it? Do you know?

DE GUICHE
Myself!—
(The laughter ceases.)
I hired them to do the sort of work
We do not soil our hands with—punishing
A drunken poet. . . .
(Uncomfortable silence)
73

THE CADET

(To CYRANO*)*

What shall we do with them?
They ought to be preserved before they spoil—

CYRANO

(Takes the sword, and in the gesture of saluting
DE GUICHE *with it, makes all the hats slide off*
at his feet.)

Sir, will you not return these to your friends?

DE GUICHE

My chair—my porters here—immediately!
(To CYRANO *violently)*
—As for you, sir!—

A VOICE

(In the street)

The chair of Monseigneur
Le Comte de Guiche!—

DE GUICHE

(Who has recovered his self-control; smiling)
Have you read *Don Quixote?*

CYRANO

I have—and found myself the hero.

A PORTER

(Appears at the door.)

Chair

Ready!

DE GUICHE

Be so good as to read once more
The chapter of the windmills.

CYRANO

(Gravely)

Chapter Thirteen.

DE GUICHE

Windmills, remember, if you fight with them—

CYRANO

My enemies change, then, with every wind?

DE GUICHE

—May swing round their huge arms and cast you down
Into the mire.

CYRANO

Or up—among the stars!
*(*DE GUICHE *goes out. We see him get into the*
chair. The Officers follow murmuring among
themselves. LE BRET *goes up with them. The*
crowd goes out.)

CYRANO

*(Saluting with burlesque politeness, those who go
out without daring to take leave of him.)*

Gentlemen. . . . Gentlemen. . . .

LE BRET

*(As the door closes, comes down, shaking his
clenched hands to heaven.)*

You have done it now—
You have made your fortune!

CYRANO

There you go again,
Growling!—

LE BRET

At least this latest pose of yours—
Ruining every chance that comes your way—
Becomes exaggerated—

CYRANO

Very well,
Then I exaggerate!

LE BRET

(Triumphantly)

Oh, you do!

CYRANO

Yes;
On principle. There are things in this world
A man does well to carry to extremes.

LE BRET

Stop trying to be Three Musketeers in one!
Fortune and glory—

CYRANO

What would you have me do?
Seek for the patronage of some great man,
And like a creeping vine on a tall tree
Crawl upward, where I cannot stand alone?
No thank you! Dedicate, as others do,
Poems to pawnbrokers? Be a buffoon
In the vile hope of teasing out a smile
On some cold face? No thank you! Eat a toad
For breakfast every morning? Make my knees
Callous, and cultivate a supple spine,—
Wear out my belly grovelling in the dust?
No thank you! Scratch the back of any swine
That roots up gold for me? Tickle the horns
Of Mammon with my left hand, while my right
Too proud to know his partner's business,

75

Takes in the fee? No thank you! Use the fire
God gave me to burn incense all day long
Under the nose of wood and stone? No thank you!
Shall I go leaping into ladies' laps
And licking fingers?—or—to change the form—
Navigating with madrigals for oars,
My sails full of the sighs of dowagers?
No thank you! Publish verses at my own
Expense? No thank you! Be the patron saint
Of a small group of literary souls
Who dine together every Tuesday? No
I thank you! Shall I labor night and day
To build a reputation on one song,
And never write another? Shall I find
True genius only among Geniuses,
Palpitate over little paragraphs,
And struggle to insinuate my name
In the columns of the *Mercury?*
No thank you! Calculate, scheme, be afraid,
Love more to make a visit than a poem,
Seek introductions, favors, influences?—
No thank you! No, I thank you! And again
I thank you!—But . . .

                        To sing, to laugh, to dream,
To walk in my own way and be alone,
Free, with an eye to see things as they are,
A voice that means manhood—to cock my hat
Where I choose— At a word, a *Yes,* a *No,*
To fight—or write. To travel any road
Under the sun, under the stars, nor doubt
If fame or fortune lie beyond the bourne—
Never to make a line I have not heard
In my own heart; yet, with all modesty
To say: "My soul, be satisfied with flowers,
With fruit, with weeds even; but gather them
In the one garden you may call your own."
So, when I win some triumph, by some chance,
Render no share to Caesar—in a word,
I am too proud to be a parasite,
And if my nature wants the germ that grows
Towering to heaven like the mountain pine,
Or like the oak, sheltering multitudes—
I stand, not high it may be—but alone!

Alone, yes!—But why stand against the world?
What devil has possessed you now, to go
Everywhere making yourself enemies?

CYRANO

Watching you other people making friends
Everywhere—as a dog makes friends! I mark
The manner of these canine courtesies
And think: "My friends are of a cleaner breed;
Here comes—thank God!—another enemy!"

LE BRET

But this is madness!

CYRANO

Method, let us say.

It is my pleasure to displease. I love
Hatred. Imagine how it feels to face
The volley of a thousand angry eyes—
The bile of envy and the froth of fear
Spattering little drops about me— You—
Good nature all around you, soft and warm—
You are like those Italians, in great cowls
Comfortable and loose— Your chin sinks down
Into the folds, your shoulders droop. But I—
The Spanish ruff I wear around my throat
Is like a ring of enemies; hard, proud,
Each point another pride, another thorn—
So that I hold myself erect perforce
Wearing the hatred of the common herd
Haughtily, the harsh collar of Old Spain,
At once a fetter and—a halo!

LE BRET

Yes . . .

(After a silence, draws CYRANO's arm through his own.)

Tell this to all the world— And then to me
Say very softly that . . . She loves you not.

CYRANO

(Quickly)

Hush!

(A moment since, CHRISTIAN has entered and mingled with the Cadets, who do not offer to speak to him. Finally, he sits down alone at a small table, where he is served by LISE.)

77

A CADET
(Rises from a table up stage, his glass in his hand.)
Cyrano!—Your story!

CYRANO
Presently . . .
(He goes up, on the arm of Le Bret, *talking to him. The Cadet comes down stage.)*

THE CADET
The story of the combat! An example
For—
(He stops by the table where Christian *is sitting.)*
—this young tadpole here.

CHRISTIAN
(Looks up)
Tadpole?

ANOTHER CADET
Yes, you!—
You narrow-gutted Northerner!

CHRISTIAN
Sir?

FIRST CADET
Hark ye,
Monsieur de Neuvillette: You are to know
There is a certain subject—I would say,
A certain object—never to be named
Among us: utterly unmentionable!

CHRISTIAN
And that is?

THIRD CADET
(In an awful voice)
Look at me! . . .
(He strikes his nose three times with his finger, mysteriously.)
You understand?

CHRISTIAN
Why, yes; the—

FOURTH CADET
Sh! . . . We never speak that word—
(Indicating Cyrano *by a gesture)*
To breathe it is to have to do with him!

FIFTH CADET
(Speaks through his nose.)
He has exterminated several
Whose tone of voice suggested . . .

78

SIXTH CADET
(In a hollow tone; rising from under the table on all fours.)

Would you die
Before your time? Just mention anything
Convex . . . or cartilaginous . . .

SEVENTH CADET
(His hand on CHRISTIAN's *shoulder)*

One word—
One syllable—one gesture—nay, one sneeze—
Your handkerchief becomes your winding-sheet!

(Silence. In a circle around CHRISTIAN, *arms crossed, they regard him expectantly.)*

CHRISTIAN
(Rises and goes to CARBON, *who is conversing with an officer, and pretending not to see what is taking place.)*

Captain!

CARBON
(Turns, and looks him over.)
Sir?

CHRISTIAN
What is the proper thing to do
When Gascons grow too boastful?

CARBON
Prove to them
That one may be a Norman, and have courage.
(Turns his back.)

CHRISTIAN
I thank you.

FIRST CADET
(To CYRANO)
Come—the story!

ALL
The story!

CYRANO
(Come down.)
Oh,
My story? Well . . .
(They all draw up their stools and group themselves around him, eagerly. CHRISTIAN *places himself astride of a chair, his arms on the back of it.)*

I marched on, all alone
To meet those devils. Overhead, the moon
Hung like a gold watch at the fob of heaven,

Till suddenly some Angel rubbed a cloud,
As it might be his handkerchief, across
The shining crystal, and—the night came down.
No lamps in those back streets— It was so dark—
Mordious! You could not see beyond—

CHRISTIAN

> Your nose.

*(Silence. Every man slowly rises to his feet. They
look at* CYRANO *almost with terror. He has
stopped short, utterly astonished. Pause.)*

CYRANO

Who is that man there?

A CADET

(In a low voice)

> A recruit—arrived

This morning.

CYRANO

(Takes a step toward CHRISTIAN.*)*
    A recruit—

CARBON

(In a low voice)

> His name is Christian

De Neuvil—

CYRANO

(Suddenly motionless)
    Oh . . .
*(He turns pale, flushes, makes a movement as if to
throw himself upon* CHRISTIAN.*)*
    I—
(Controls himself, and goes on in a choking voice.)

> I see. Very well,

As I was saying—
(With a sudden burst of rage)
    Mordious! . . .
(He goes on in a natural tone.)

> It grew dark,

You could not see your hand before your eyes.
I marched on, thinking how, all for the sake
Of one old souse
(They slowly sit down, watching him.)
    who wrote a bawdy song
Whenever he took—

CHRISTIAN
A noseful—

80

*(Everyone rises. CHRISTIAN balances himself on
two legs of his chair.)*

CYRANO

(Half strangled)

—Took a notion.

Whenever he took a notion— For his sake,
I might antagonize some dangerous man,
One powerful enough to make me pay—

CHRISTIAN

Through the nose—

CYRANO

(Wipes the sweat from his forehead.)

—Pay the Piper. After all,
I thought, why am I putting in my—

CHRISTIAN

Nose—

CYRANO

—My oar ... Why am I putting in my oar?
The quarrel's none of mine. However—now
I am here, I may as well go through with it.
Come Gascon—do your duty!—Suddenly
A sword flashed in the dark. I caught it fair—

CHRISTIAN

On the nose—

CYRANO

On my blade. Before I knew it,
There I was—

CHRISTIAN

Rubbing noses—

CYRANO

(Pale and smiling)

Crossing swords

With half a score at once. I handed one—

CHRISTIAN

A nosegay—

CYRANO

(Leaping at him)

Ventre-Saint-Gris! ...

*(The Gascons tumble over each other to get a good
view. Arrived in front of CHRISTIAN, who has
not moved an inch, CYRANO masters himself
again, and continues.)*

He went down;

The rest gave way; I charged—

81

CHRISTIAN

Nose in the air—

CYRANO

I skewered two of them—disarmed a third—
Another lunged— Paf! And I countered—

CHRISTIAN

Pif!

CYRANO

(Bellowing)
TONNERRE! Out of here!—All of you!
(All the Cadets rush for the door.)

FIRST CADET

At last—

The old lion wakes!

CYRANO

All of you! Leave me here
Alone with that man!
*(The lines following are heard brokenly in the con-
fusion of getting through the door.)*

SECOND CADET

Bigre! He'll have the fellow
Chopped into sausage—

RAGUENEAU

Sausage?—

THIRD CADET

Mince-meat, then—

One of your pies!—

RAGUENEAU

Am I pale? You look white
As a fresh napkin—

CARBON *(At the door)*
Come!

FOURTH CADET

He'll never leave
Enough of him to—

FIFTH CADET

Why, it frightens ME
To think of what will—

SIXTH CADET

(Closing the door)
Something horrible
Beyond imagination . . .
*(They are all gone: some through the street door,
some by the inner doors to right and left. A few*

82

disappear up the staircase. CYRANO *and* CHRIS-
TIAN *stand face to face a moment, and look at
each other.)*

CYRANO

To my arms!

CHRISTIAN

Sir?...

CYRANO

You have courage!

CHRISTIAN

Oh, that!...

CYRANO

You are brave—

That pleases me.

CHRISTIAN

You mean?...

CYRANO

Do you not know

I am her brother? Come!

CHRISTIAN

Whose?—

CYRANO

Hers—Roxane!

CHRISTIAN

Her ... brother? You? *(Hurries to him.)*

CYRANO

Her cousin. Much the same.

CHRISTIAN

And she has told you?...

CYRANO

Everything.

CHRISTIAN

She loves me?

CYRANO

Perhaps.

CHRISTIAN
(Takes both his hands.)
My dear sir—more than I can say,

I am honored—

CYRANO

This is rather sudden.

CHRISTIAN

Please

Forgive me—

CYRANO
(Holds him at arm's length, looking at him.)
Why, he is a handsome devil.

This fellow!

CHRISTIAN
On my honor—if you knew
How much I have admired—

CYRANO
Yes, yes—and all

Those Noses which—

CHRISTIAN
Please! I apologize.

CYRANO *(Change of tone)*
Roxane expects a letter—

CHRISTIAN
Not from me?—

CYRANO
Yes. Why not?

CHRISTIAN
Once I write, that ruins all!

CYRANO
And why?

CHRISTIAN
Because . . . because I am a fool!
Stupid enough to hang myself!

CYRANO
But no—
You are no fool; you call yourself a fool,
There's proof enough in that. Besides, you did not
Attack me like a fool.

CHRISTIAN
Bah! Any one
Can pick a quarrel. Yes, I have a sort
Of rough and ready soldier's tongue. I know
That. But with any woman—paralyzed,
Speechless, dumb. I can only look at them.
Yet sometimes, when I go away, their eyes . . .

CYRANO
Why not their hearts, if you should wait and see?

CHRISTIAN
No. I am one of those— I know—those men
Who never can make love.

CYRANO
Strange. . . . Now it seems

I, if I gave my mind to it, I might
Perhaps make love well.

CHRISTIAN

Oh, if I had words

To say what I have here!

CYRANO

If I could be

A handsome little Musketeer with eyes!—

CHRISTIAN

Besides—you know Roxane—how sensitive—
One rough word, and the sweet illusion—gone!

CYRANO

I wish you might be my interpreter.

CHRISTIAN

I wish I had your wit—

CYRANO

Borrow it, then!—

Your beautiful young manhood—lend me that,
And we two make one hero of romance!

CHRISTIAN

What?

CYRANO

Would you dare repeat to her the words

I gave you, day by day?

CHRISTIAN

You mean?

CYRANO

I mean

Roxane shall have no disillusionment!
Come, shall we win her both together? Take
The soul within this learthern jack of mine,
And breathe it into you?

(Touches him on the breast.)

So—there's my heart

Under your velvet, now!

CHRISTIAN

But— Cyrano!—

CYRANO

But— Christian, why not?

CHRISTIAN

I am afraid—

CYRANO

I know—

Afraid that when you have her all alone,

85

You lose all. Have no fear. It is yourself
She loves—give her yourself put into words—
My words, upon your lips!

                    CHRISTIAN
                              But . . . but your eyes! . . .

They burn like—

                    CYRANO
                    Will you? . . . Will you?
                    CHRISTIAN
                                        Does it mean

So much to you?
                    CYRANO *(Beside himself)*
                              It means—
                    (Recovers, changes tone.)
                                        A Comedy,

A situation for a poet! Come.
Shall we collaborate? I'll be your cloak
Of darkness, your enchanted sword, your ring
To charm the fairy Princess!

                    CHRISTIAN
                              But the letter—

I cannot write—

                    CYRANO
                    Oh yes, the letter.
                    *(He takes from his pocket the letter which he has
                    written.)*
                                        Here.

                    CHRISTIAN
What is this?

                    CYRANO
                    All there; all but the address.
                    CHRISTIAN

I—

                    CYRANO
                    Oh, you may send it. It will serve.
                    CHRISTIAN
                                        But why

Have you done this?

                    CYRANO
                              I have amused myself

As we all do, we poets—writing vows
To Chloris, Phyllis—any pretty name—
You might have had a pocketful of them!
Take it, and turn to facts my fantasies—

I loosed these loves like doves into the air;
Give them a habitation and a home.
Here, take it— You will find me all the more
Eloquent, being insincere! Come!

CHRISTIAN

First,
There must be a few changes here and there—
Written at random, can it fit Roxane?

CYRANO

Like her own glove.

CHRISTIAN

No, but—

CYRANO

My son, have faith—
Faith in the love of women for themselves—
Roxane will know this letter for her own!

CHRISTIAN

(Throws himself into the arms of CYRANO. *They
stand embraced.)*

My friend!

(The door up stage opens a little. A Cadet steals in.)

THE CADET

Nothing. A silence like the tomb . . .
I hardly dare look— *(He sees the two.)*

Wha-at?

(The other Cadets crowd in behind him and see.)

THE CADETS

No!—No!

SECOND CADET

Mon dieu!

THE MUSKETEER

(Slaps his knee.)

Well, well, well!

CARBON

Here's our devil . . . Christianized!
Offend one nostril, and he turns the other.

THE MUSKETEER

Now we are allowed to talk about his nose! *(Calls)*
Hey, Lise! Come here— *(Affectedly)*

Snf! What a horrid smell!
What is it? . . .

(Plants himself in front of CYRANO, *and looks at his
nose in an impolite manner.)*

You ought to know about such things;
What seems to have died around here?

87

CYRANO

(Knocks him backward over a bench.)

Cabbage-heads!

(Joy. The Cadets have found their old CYRANO *again. General disturbance.)*

(Curtain)

THE THIRD ACT

ROXANE'S KISS

A little square in the old Marais: old houses, and a glimpse of narrow streets. On the Right, THE HOUSE OF ROXANE and her garden wall, overhung with tall shrubbery. Over the door of the house a balcony and a tall window; to one side of the door, a bench.

Ivy clings to the wall; jasmine embraces the balcony, trembles, and falls away.

By the bench and the jutting stonework of the wall one might easily climb up to the balcony.

Opposite, an ancient house of the like character, brick and stone, whose front door forms an Entrance. The knocker on this door is tied up in linen like an injured thumb.

At the CURTAIN RISE the Duenna is seated on the bench beside the door. The window is wide open on ROXANE'S balcony; a light within suggests that it is early evening. By the Duenna stands RAGUENEAU dressed in what might be the livery of one attached to the household. He is by way of telling her something, and wiping his eyes meanwhile.

RAGUENEAU

—And so she ran off with a Musketeer!
I was ruined—I was alone— Remained
Nothing for me to do but hang myself,
So I did that. Presently along comes
Monsieur de Bergerac, and cuts me down,
And makes me steward to his cousin.

THE DUENNA

Ruined?—

I thought your pastry was a great success!

RAGUENEAU

(Shakes his head.)

Lise loved the soldiers, and I loved the poets—
Mars ate up all the cakes Apollo left;
It did not take long. . . .

89

THE DUENNA
(Calls up to window.)

Roxane! Are you ready?
We are late!

VOICE OF ROXANE
(Within)

Putting on my cape—

THE DUENNA
(To RAGUENEAU, *indicating the house opposite.)*

Clomire
Across the way receives on Thursday nights—
We are to have a psycho-colioquy
Upon the Tender Passion.

RAGUENEAU

Ah—the Tender . . .

THE DUENNA
(Sighs)

—Passion! . . .
(Calls up to window.)

Roxane!—Hurry, dear—we shall miss
The Tender Passion!

ROXANE

Coming!—
(Music of stringed instruments off-stage approaching.)

THE VOICE OF CYRANO
(Singing)

La, la, la!—

THE DUENNA
A serenade?—How pleasant—

CYRANO

No, no, no!—
F natural, you natural born fool!
(Enters, followed by two pages, carrying theorbos.)

FIRST PAGE
(Ironically)
No doubt your honor knows F natural
When he hears—

CYRANO

I am a musician, infant!—
A pupil of Gassendi.

THE PAGE
(Plays and sings.)
La, la,—

90

Here—

Give me that—

(He snatches the instrument from the Page and continues the tune.)

La, la, la, la—

ROXANE

(Appears on the balcony.)

Is that you,
Cyrano?

CYRANO

(Singing)

I, who praise your lilies fair,
But long to love your ro . . . ses!

ROXANE

I'll be down—

Wait—

(Goes in through window.)

THE DUENNA

Did you train these virtuosi?

CYRANO

No—

I won them on a bet from D'Assoucy.
We were debating a fine point of grammar
When, pointing out these two young nightingales
Dressed up like peacocks, with their instruments,
He cries: "No, but I KNOW! I'll wager you
A day of music." Well, of course he lost;
And so until to-morrow they are mine,
My private orchestra. Pleasant at first,
But they become a trifle—

(To the Pages)

Here! Go play

A minuet to Montfleury—and tell him
I sent you!

(The Pages go up to the exit. CYRANO *turns to the Duenna)*

I came here as usual

To inquire after our friend—

(To Pages)

Play out of tune.

And keep on playing!

(The Pages go out. He turns to the Duenna)

Our friend with the great soul.

ROXANE

(Enters in time to hear the last words.)

He is beautiful and brilliant—and I love him!

CYRANO

Do you find Christian . . . intellectual?

ROXANE

More so than you, even.

CYRANO

I am glad.

ROXANE

No man

Ever so beautifully said those things—
Those pretty nothings that are everything.
Sometimes he falls into a reverie;
His inspiration fails—then all at once,
He will say something absolutely . . . Oh! . . .

CYRANO

Really!

ROXANE

How like a man! You think a man
Who has a handsome face must be a fool.

CYRANO

He talks well about . . . matters of the heart?

ROXANE

He does not *talk;* he rhapsodizes . . . dreams . . .

CYRANO

(Twisting his moustache.)

He . . . writes well?

ROXANE

Wonderfully. Listen now:

(Reciting as from memory.)

"Take my heart; I shall have it all the more;
Plucking the flowers, we keep the plant in bloom—"
Well?

CYRANO

Pooh!

ROXANE

And this:

"Knowing you have in store
More heart to give than I to find heart-room—"

CYRANO

First he has too much, then too little; just
How much heart does he need?

92

ROXANE

(Tapping her foot.)

You are teasing me!

You are jealous!

CYRANO

(Startled)

Jealous?

ROXANE

Of his poetry—

You poets are like that . . .

And these last lines
Are they not the last word in tenderness?—
"There is no more to say: only believe
That unto you my whole heart gives one cry,
And writing, writes down more than you receive;
Sending you kisses through my finger-tips—
Lady, O read my letter with your lips!"

CYRANO

H'm, yes— those last lines . . . but he overwrites!

ROXANE

Listen to this—

CYRANO

You know them all by heart?

ROXANE

Every one!

CYRANO

(Twisting his moustache.)

I may call that flattering . . .

ROXANE

He is a master!

CYRANO

Oh—come!

ROXANE

Yes—a master!

CYRANO

(Bowing)

A master—if you will!

THE DUENNA

(Comes down stage quickly.)

Monsieur de Guiche!—

(To CYRANO, pushing him toward the house.)

Go inside— If he does not find you here,
It may be just as well. He may suspect—

ROXANE

—My secret! Yes; he is in love with me
And he is powerful. Let him not know—
One look would frost my roses before bloom.

CYRANO

(Going into house.)

Very well, very well!

ROXANE

(To DE GUICHE, *as he enters)*

We were just going—

DE GUICHE

I came only to say farewell.

ROXANE

You leave

Paris?

DE GUICHE

Yes—for the front.

ROXANE

Ah!

DE GUICHE

And to-night!

ROXANE

Ah!

DE GUICHE

We have orders to besiege Arras.

ROXANE

Arras?

DE GUICHE

Yes. My departure leaves you . . . cold?

ROXANE

(Politely)

Oh! Not that.

DE GUICHE

It has left me desolate—
When shall I see you? Ever? Did you know
I was made Colonel?

ROXANE

(Indifferent)

Bravo.

DE GUICHE

Regiment

Of the Guards.

ROXANE

(Catching her breath.)

Of the Guards?—

His regiment

Your cousin, the mighty man of words!—
> *(Grimly)*

Down there

We may have an accounting!

ROXANE
> *(Suffocating)*

Are you sure

The Guards are ordered?

DE GUICHE

Under my command!

ROXANE
> *(Sinks down, breathless, on the bench; aside)*

Christian!—

DE GUICHE

What is it?

ROXANE
> *(Losing control of herself.)*

To the war—perhaps

Never again to— When a woman cares,
Is that nothing?

DE GUICHE
> *(Surprised and delighted.)*

You say this now—to me—

Now, at the very moment?—

ROXANE
> *(Recovers—changes her tone.)*

Tell me something:

My cousin— You say you mean to be revenged
On him. Do you mean that?

DE GUICHE

> *(Smiles)*

Why? Would you care?

ROXANE

Not for him.

DE GUICHE

Do you see him?

ROXANE

Now and then.

DE GUICHE

He goes about everywhere nowadays
With one of the Cadets—de Neuve—Neuville—
Neuvillers—

ROXANE

(Coolly)

A tall man?—

DE GUICHE

Blond—

ROXANE

Rosy cheeks?—

DE GUICHE

Handsome!—

ROXANE

Pooh!—

DE GUICHE

And a fool.

ROXANE

(Languidly)

So he appears . . .

(Animated)

But Cyrano? What will you do to him?
Order him into danger? He loves that!
I know what *I* should do.

DE GUICHE

What?

ROXANE

Leave him here

With his Cadets, while all the regiment
Goes on to glory! That would torture him—
To sit all through the war with folded arms—
I know his nature. If you hate that man,
Strike at his self-esteem.

DE GUICHE

Oh woman—woman!

Who but a woman would have thought of this?

ROXANE

He'll eat his heart out, while his Gascon friends
Bite their nails all day long in Paris here.
And you will be avenged!

DE GUICHE

You love me then,

A little? . . . *(She smiles.)*

Making my enemies your own,
Hating them—I should like to see in that
A sign of love, Roxane.

ROXANE

Perhaps it is one . . .

DE GUICHE

(Shows a number of folded despatches.)

Here are the orders—for each company—
Ready to send . . .

(Selects one.)

So— This is for the Guards—

I'll keep that. Aha, Cyrano!

(To ROXANE)

You too,

You play your little games, do you?

ROXANE

(Watching him.)

Sometimes . . .

DE GUICHE

(Close to her, speaking hurriedly.)

And you!—Oh, I am mad over you!—

Listen—

I leave to-night—but—let you through my hands
Now, when I feel you trembling?—Listen— Close by,
In the Rue d'Orléans, the Capuchins
Have their new convent. By their law, no layman
May pass inside those walls. I'll see to that—
Their sleeves are wide enough to cover me—
The servants of my Uncle-Cardinal
Will fear his nephew. So—I'll come to you
Masked, after everyone knows I have gone—
Oh, let me wait one day!—

ROXANE

If this be known,

Your honor—

DE GUICHE

Bah!

ROXANE

The war—your duty—

DE GUICHE

(Blows away an imaginary feather.)

Phoo!—

Only say yes!

ROXANE

No!

DE GUICHE

Whisper . . .

ROXANE

(Tenderly)

97

I ought not

To let you . . .

DE GUICHE

Ah! . . .

ROXANE

(Pretends to break down.)

Ah, go!

(Aside)

—Christian remains—

(Aloud—heroically)

I must have you a hero—Antoine . . .

DE GUICHE

Heaven! . . .

So you can love—

ROXANE

One for whose sake I fear.

DE GUICHE

(Triumphant)

I go!

Will that content you?
(Kisses her hand.)

ROXANE

Yes—my friend!

(He goes out.)

THE DUENNA

(As DE GUICHE *disappears, making a deep curtsey behind his back, and imitating* ROXANE's *intense tone.)*

Yes—my friend!

ROXANE

(Quickly, close to her.)

Not a word to Cyrano—

He would never forgive me if he knew
I stole his war!

(She calls toward the house.)

Cousin!

*(*CYRANO *comes out of the house; she turns to him, indicating the house opposite.)*

We are going over—

Alcandre speaks to-night—and Lysimon.

THE DUENNA

(Puts finger in her ear.)

My little finger says we shall not hear
Everything.

98

CYRANO

Never mind me—

THE DUENNA

(Across the street)

Look— Oh, look!

The knocker tied up in a napkin— Yes,
They muzzled you because you bark too loud
And interrupt the lecture—little beast!

ROXANE

(As the door opens)

Enter . . .

(To CYRANO)

If Christian comes, tell him to wait.

CYRANO

Oh—

(ROXANE returns.)

When he comes, what will you talk about?
You always know beforehand.

ROXANE

About . . .

CYRANO

Well?

ROXANE

You will not tell him, will you?

CYRANO

I am dumb.

ROXANE

About nothing! Or about everything—
I shall say: "Speak of love in your own words—
Improvise! Rhapsodize! Be eloquent!"

CYRANO

(Smiling)

Good!

ROXANE

Sh!—

CYRANO

Sh!—

ROXANE

Not a word!

(She goes in; the door closes.)

CYRANO

(Bowing)

Thank you so much—

ROXANE

(Opens door and puts out her head.)

He must be unprepared—

CYRANO

Of course!

ROXANE

Sh!—

(Goes in again.)

CYRANO

(Calls)

Christian!

(CHRISTIAN enters.)

I have your theme—bring on your memory!—
Here is your chance now to surpass yourself,
No time to lose— Come! Look intelligent—
Come home and learn your lines.

CHRISTIAN

No.

CYRANO

What?

CHRISTIAN

I'll wait

Here for Roxane.

CYRANO

What lunacy is this?

Come quickly!

CHRISTIAN

No, I say! I have had enough—

Taking my words, my letters, all from you—
Making our love a little comedy!
It was a game at first; but now—she cares . . .
Thanks to you. I am not afraid. I'll speak
For myself now.

CYRANO

Undoubtedly!

CHRISTIAN

I will!

Why not? I am no such fool—you shall see!
Besides—my dear friend—you have taught me much.
I ought to know something . . . By God, I know
Enough to take a woman in my arms!

(ROXANE appears in the doorway, opposite.)

There she is now . . . Cyrano, wait! Stay here!

CYRANO

(Bows)

Speak for yourself, my friend!
          (He goes out.)
                    ROXANE
          (Taking leave of the company.)
                                        —Barthénoïde!
Alcandre! . . . Grémione! . . .
                    THE DUENNA
                                        I told you so—
We missed the Tender Passion!
          (She goes into ROXANE's *house.)*
                    ROXANE
                                        Urimédonte!—
Adieu!
          *(As the guests disappear down the street, she turns
          to* CHRISTIAN.*)*
                    Is that you, Christian? Let us stay
Here, in the twilight. They are gone. The air
Is fragrant. We shall be alone. Sit down
There—so . . .
          (They sit on the bench.)
                    Now tell me things.
                    CHRISTIAN
          (After a silence)
                                        I love you.
                    ROXANE
          (Closes her eyes.)
                                                  Yes,
Speak to me about love . . .
                    CHRISTIAN
                                        I love you.
                    ROXANE
                                                  Now
Be eloquent! . . .
                    CHRISTIAN
                    I love—
                    ROXANE
          (Opens her eyes.)
                                        You have your theme—
Improvise! Rhapsodize!
                    CHRISTIAN
                                        I love you so!
                    ROXANE
Of course. And then? . . .
                    CHRISTIAN
                              And then . . . Oh, I should be
                    101

So happy if you loved me too! Roxane,
Say that you love me too!

ROXANE

(Making a face.)

I ask for cream
You give me milk and water. Tell me first
A little, how you love me.

CHRISTIAN

Very much.

ROXANE

Oh—tell me how you *feel!*

CHRISTIAN

(Coming nearer, and devouring her with his eyes.)

Your throat . . . If only
I might . . . kiss it—

ROXANE

Christian!

CHRISTIAN

I love you so!

ROXANE

(Makes as if to rise.)

Again?

CHRISTIAN

(Desperately, restraining her.)

No, not again— I do not love you—

ROXANE

(Settles back.)

That is better . . .

CHRISTIAN

I adore you!

ROXANE

Oh!—

(Rises and moves away.)

CHRISTIAN

I know;
I grow absurd.

ROXANE

(Coldly)

And that displeases me
As much as if you had grown ugly.

CHRISTIAN

I—

ROXANE

Gather your dreams together into words!

102

CHRISTIAN

I love—

ROXANE

I know; you love me. Adieu.
(She goes to the house.)

CHRISTIAN

No,

But wait—please—let me— I was going to say—

ROXANE

(Pushes the door open.)

That you adore me. Yes; I know that too.
No! . . . Go away! . . .

(She goes in and shuts the door in his face.)

CHRISTIAN

I . . . I . . .

CYRANO

(Enters)

A great success!

CHRISTIAN

Help me!

CYRANO

Not I.

CHRISTIAN

I cannot live unless
She loves me—now, this moment!

CYRANO

How the devil

Am I to teach you now—this moment?

CHRISTIAN

(Catches him by the arm.)

—Wait!—

Look! Up there!—Quick—

(The light shows in ROXANE's window.)

CYRANO

Her window—

CHRISTIAN

(Wailing)

I shall die!—

CYRANO

Less noise!

CHRISTIAN

Oh, I—

CYRANO

It does seem fairly dark—

103

(Excitedly)
Well?—Well?—Well?—

CYRANO

Let us try what can be done;
It is more than you deserve—stand over there,
Idiot—there!—before the balcony—
Let me stand underneath. I'll whisper you
What to say.

CHRISTIAN
She may hear—she may—

CYRANO

Less noise!

(The Pages appear up stage.)

FIRST PAGE

Hep!—

CYRANO

(Finger to lips)
Sh!—

FIRST PAGE

(Low voice)
We serenaded Montfleury!—
What next?

CYRANO

Down to the corner of the street—
One this way—and the other over there—
If anybody passes, play a tune!

PAGE

What tune, O musical Philosopher?

CYRANO

Sad for a man, or merry for a woman—
Now go!

(The Pages disappear, one toward each corner of the street.)

CYRANO

(To CHRISTIAN)
Call her!

CHRISTIAN
Roxane!

CYRANO
Wait . . .
(Gathers up a handful of pebbles.)

Gravel . . .

(Throws it at the window)

There!—

ROXANE

(Opens the window.)

Who is calling?

CHRISTIAN

I—

ROXANE

Who?

CHRISTIAN

Christian.

ROXANE

You again?

CHRISTIAN

I had to tell you—

CYRANO

(Under the balcony)

Good— Keep your voice down.

ROXANE

No. Go away. You tell me nothing.

CHRISTIAN

Please!—

ROXANE

You do not love me any more—

CHRISTIAN

(To whom CYRANO whispers his words)

No—no—

Not any more— I love you . . . evermore . . .

And ever . . . more and more!

ROXANE

(About to close the window—pauses.)

A little better . . .

CHRISTIAN

(Same business)

Love grows and struggles like . . . an angry child . . .

Breaking my heart . . . his cradle . . .

ROXANE

(Coming out on the balcony.)

Better still—

But . . . such a babe is dangerous; why not

Have smothered it new-born?

CHRISTIAN

(Same business)

And so I do . . .

And yet he lives . . . I found . . . as you shall find . . .

This new-born babe . . . an infant . . . Hercules!

ROXANE

(Further forward)

Good!—

CHRISTIAN

(Same business)

Strong enough ... at birth ... to strangle those
Two serpents—Doubt and ... Pride.

ROXANE

(Leans over balcony.)

Why, very well!

Tell me now why you speak so haltingly—
Has your imagination gone lame?

CYRANO

*(Thrusts CHRISTIAN under the balcony, and stands
in his place.)*

Here—

This grows too difficult!

ROXANE

Your words to-night

Hesitate. Why?

CYRANO

(In a low tone, imitating CHRISTIAN)

Through the warm summer gloom
They grope in darkness toward the light of you.

ROXANE

My words, well aimed, find you more readily.

CYRANO

My heart is open wide and waits for them—
Too large a mark to miss! My words fly home,
Heavy with honey like returning bees,
To your small secret ear. Moreover—yours
Fall to me swiftly. Mine more slowly rise.

ROXANE

Yet not so slowly as they did at first.

CYRANO

They have learned the way, and you have welcomed them.

ROXANE

(Softly)

Am I so far above you now?

CYRANO

So far—

If you let fall upon me one hard word,
Out of that height—you crush me!

106

ROXANE

(Turns)

I'll come down—

CYRANO

(Quickly)

No!

ROXANE

(Points out the bench under the balcony.)
Stand you on the bench. Come nearer!

CYRANO

(Recoils into the shadow.)

No!—

ROXANE

And why—so great a *No?*

CYRANO

(More and more overcome by emotion.)

Let me enjoy

The one moment I ever—my one chance
To speak to you . . . unseen!

ROXANE

Unseen?—

CYRANO

Yes!—yes . . .

Night, making all things dimly beautiful,
One veil over us both— You only see
The darkness of a long cloak in the gloom,
And I the whiteness of a summer gown—
You are all light— I am all shadow! . . . How
Can you know what this moment means to me?
If I was ever eloquent—

ROXANE

You were

Eloquent—

CYRANO

—You have never heard till now

My own heart speaking!

ROXANE

Why not?

CYRANO

Until now,

I spoke through . . .

ROXANE

Yes?—

CYRANO

—through that sweet drunkenness
You pour into the world out of your eyes!
But to-night . . . but to-night, I indeed speak
For the first time!

ROXANE

For the first time— Your voice,
Even, is not the same.

CYRANO

(Passionately; moves nearer.)

How should it be?
I have another voice—my own,
Myself, daring—

(He stops, confused; then tries to recover himself.)

Where was I? . . . I forget! . . .
Forgive me. This is all sweet like a dream . . .
Strange—like a dream . . .

ROXANE

How, strange?

CYRANO

Is it not so
To be myself to you, and have no fear
Of moving you to laughter?

ROXANE

Laughter—why?

CYRANO

(Struggling for an explanation)

Because . . . What am I . . . What is any man,
That he dare ask for you? Therefore my heart
Hides behind phrases. There's a modesty
In these things too— I come here to pluck down
Out of the sky the evening star—then smile,
And stoop to gather little flowers.

ROXANE

Are they
Not sweet, those little flowers?

CYRANO

Not enough sweet
For you and me, to-night!

ROXANE

(Breathless)

You never spoke
To me like this . . .

CYRANO

Little things, pretty things—

Arrows and hearts and torches—roses red,
And violets blue—are these all? Come away,
And breathe fresh air! Must we keep on and on
Sipping stale honey out of tiny cups
Decorated with golden tracery,
Drop by drop, all day long? We are alive;
We thirst— Come away, plunge, and drink, and drown
In the great river flowing to the sea!

ROXANE

But . . . Poetry?

CYRANO

            I have made rimes for you—
Not now— Shall we insult Nature, this night,
These flowers, this moment—shall we set all these
To phrases from a letter by Voiture?
Look once at the high stars that shine in heaven,
And put off artificiality!
Have you not seen great gaudy hothouse flowers,
Barren, without fragrance?—Souls are like that:
Forced to show all, they soon become all show—
The means to Nature's end ends meaningless!

ROXANE

But . . . Poetry?

CYRANO

               Love hates that game of words!
It is a crime to fence with life— I tell you,
There comes one moment, once—and God help those
Who pass that moment by!—when Beauty stands
Looking into the soul with grave, sweet eyes
That sicken at pretty words!

ROXANE

                 If that be true—
And when that moment comes to you and me—
What words will you? . . .

CYRANO

             All those, all those, all those
That blossom in my heart, I'll fling to you—
Armfuls of loose bloom! Love, I love beyond
Breath, beyond reason, beyond love's own power
Of loving! Your name is like a golden bell
Hung in my heart; and when I think of you,
I tremble, and the bell swings and rings—

                     "Roxane!" . . .
"Roxane!" . . . along my veins, "Roxane!" . . .

                       I know

109

All small forgotten things that once meant You—
I remember last year, the First of May,
A little before noon, you had your hair
Drawn low, that one time only. Is that strange?
You know how, after looking at the sun,
One sees red suns everywhere—so, for hours
After the flood of sunshine that you are,
My eyes are blinded by your burning hair!

ROXANE

(Very low)

Yes ... that is ... Love—

CYRANO

                    Yes, that is Love—that wind
Of terrible and jealous beauty, blowing
Over me—that dark fire, that music ...

                                  Yet

Love seeketh not his own! Dear, you may take
My happiness to make you happier,
Even though you never know I gave it you—
Only let me hear sometimes, all alone,
The distant laughter of your joy! ...

                                I never

Look at you, but there's some new virtue born
In me, some new courage. Do you begin
To understand, a little? Can you feel
My soul, there in the darkness, breathe on you?
—Oh, but to-night, now, I dare say these things—
I ... to you ... and you hear them! ... It is too much!
In my most sweet unreasonable dreams,
I have not hoped for this! Now let me die,
Having lived. It is my voice, mine, my own,
That makes you tremble there in the green gloom
Above me—for you do tremble, as a blossom
Among the leaves— You tremble, and I can feel,
All the way down along these jasmine branches,
Whether you will or no, the passion of you
Trembling ...

(He kisses wildly the end of a drooping spray of
jasmine.)

ROXANE

                    Yes, I do tremble ... and I weep ...
And I love you ... and I am yours ... and you
Have made me thus!

CYRANO

(After a pause; quietly)

What is death like, I wonder?

I know everything else now . . .

I have done

This, to you—I, myself . . .

Only let me

Ask one thing more—

CHRISTIAN

(Under the balcony)

One kiss!

ROXANE

(Startled)

One?—

CYRANO

(To CHRISTIAN*)*

You! . . .

ROXANE

You ask me

For—

CYRANO

I . . . Yes, but—I mean—

(To CHRISTIAN*)*

You go too far!

CHRISTIAN

She is willing!— Why not make the most of it?

CYRANO

(To ROXANE*)*

I did ask . . . but I know I ask too much . . .

ROXANE

Only one— Is that all?

CYRANO

All!—How much more

Than all!—I know—I frighten you—I ask . . .
I ask you to refuse—

CHRISTIAN

(To CYRANO*)*

But why? Why? Why?

CYRANO

Christian, be quiet!

ROXANE

(Leaning over.)

What is that you say

To yourself?

CYRANO

I am angry with myself

Because I go too far, and so I say

111

To myself: "Christian, be quiet!"—
             (The theorbos begin to play.)

                                        Hark—someone

Is coming—
             (ROXANE *closes her window.* CYRANO *listens to the*
                theorbos, one of which plays a gay melody, the
                other a mournful one.)
             A sad tune, a merry tune—
Man, woman—what do they mean?—
             (A Capuchin enters; he carries a lantern, and goes
                from house to house, looking at the doors.)
                                        Aha!—a priest!

        (To the Capuchin)
What is this new game of Diogenes?
                        THE CAPUCHIN
I am looking for the house of Madame—
                        CHRISTIAN
        (Impatient)

                                        Bah!—

                 THE CAPUCHIN
Madeleine Robin—
                        CHRISTIAN
                        What does he want?
                        CYRANO
        (To the Capuchin; points out a street.)

                                        This way—

To the right—keep to the right—
                 THE CAPUCHIN

                                I thank you, sir!—
I'll say my beads for you to the last grain.
                        CYRANO
Good fortune, father, and my service to you!
        (The Capuchin goes out)
                        CHRISTIAN

Win me that kiss!

                 CYRANO
                 No.
                 CHRISTIAN

                                Sooner or later—

                 CYRANO

                                        True . . .

That is true . . . Soon or late, it will be so
Because you are young and she is beautiful—
        (To himself)
Since it must be, I had rather be myself

                     112

(The window re-opens. CHRISTIAN hides under the balcony.)

The cause of . . . what must be.

ROXANE

(Out on the balcony)

Are you still there?

We were speaking of—

CYRANO

A kiss. The word is sweet—
What will the deed be? Are your lips afraid
Even of its burning name? Not much afraid—
Not too much! Have you not unwittingly
Laid aside laughter, slipping beyond speech
Insensibly, already, without fear,
From words to smiles . . . from smiles to sighs . . . from
    sighing,
Even to tears? One step more—only one—
From a tear to a kiss—one step, one thrill!

ROXANE

Hush—

CYRANO

And what is a kiss, when all is done?
A promise given under seal—a vow
Taken before the shrine of memory—
A signature acknowledged—a rosy dot
Over the i of Loving—a secret whispered
To listening lips apart—a moment made
Immortal, with a rush of wings unseen—
A sacrament of blossoms, a new song
Sung by two hearts to an old simple tune—
The ring of one horizon around two souls
Together, all alone!

ROXANE

Hush! . . .

CYRANO

Why, what shame?—
There was a Queen of France, not long ago,
And a great lord of England—a queen's gift,
A crown jewel!

ROXANE

Indeed!

CYRANO

Indeed, like him,
I have my sorrows and my silences;
Like her, you are the queen I dare adore;

113

Like him I am faithful and forlorn—

ROXANE

                                        Like him,

Beautiful—

CYRANO

(Aside)
        So I am—I forgot that!

ROXANE

Then— Come; . . . Gather your sacred blossom . . .

CYRANO

(To CHRISTIAN)

                                        Go!—

ROXANE

Your crown jewel . . .

CYRANO
        Go on!—

ROXANE

                        Your old new song . . .

CYRANO

Climb!—

CHRISTIAN

(Hesitates)
        No— Would you?—not yet—

ROXANE

                        Your moment made

Immortal . . .

CYRANO

(Pushing him.)
        Climb up, animal!
*(CHRISTIAN springs on the bench, and climbs by
    the pillars, the branches, the vines, until he be-
    strides the balcony railing.)*

CHRISTIAN

                                Roxane! . . .
(He takes her in his arms and bends over her.)

CYRANO

(Very low)
Ah! . . . Roxane! . . .

                        I have won what I have won—
The feast of love—and I am Lazarus!
Yet . . . I have something here that is mine now
And was not mine before I spoke the words
That won her—not for me! . . . Kissing my words
My words, upon your lips!
        (The theorbos begin to play.)

114

                                A merry tune—
A sad tune— So! The Capuchin!
            *(He pretends to be running, as if he had arrived
            from a distance; then calls up to the balcony.)*
                                        Hola!

                            ROXANE

Who is it?

                            CYRANO
                            I. Is Christian there with you?
                            CHRISTIAN
            (Astonished)

Cyrano!

                            ROXANE
                    Good morrow, Cousin!
                            CYRANO
                                        Cousin, . . . good morrow!
                            ROXANE

I am coming down.
            *(She disappears into the house. The Capuchin en-
            ters up stage.)*
                            CHRISTIAN
            (Sees him.)
                            Oh—again!
                        THE CAPUCHIN
            (To CYRANO*)*
                                        She lives *here,*

Madeleine Robin!

                            CYRANO
                    You said RO-LIN.
                        THE CAPUCHIN
                                            No—

R-O-B-I-N

                            ROXANE
            *(Appears on the threshold of the house, followed
            by* RAGUENEAU *with a lantern, and by* CHRIS-
            TIAN*.)*
                    What is it?
                        THE CAPUCHIN
                        A letter.
                            CHRISTIAN
                                            Oh! . . .

                        THE CAPUCHIN
            (To ROXANE*)*
Some matter profitable to the soul—
A very noble lord gave it to me!

                            115

ROXANE

(To CHRISTIAN*)*

De Guiche!

CHRISTIAN

He dares?—

ROXANE

It will not be for long;
When he learns that I love you . . .

(By the light of the lantern which RAGUENEAU
*holds, she reads the letter in a low tone, as if to
herself.)*

"Mademoiselle

The drums are beating, and the regiment
Arms for the march. Secretly I remain
Here, in the Convent. I have disobeyed;
I shall be with you soon. I send this first
By an old monk, as simple as a sheep,
Who understands nothing of this. Your smile
Is more than I can bear, and seek no more.
Be alone to-night, waiting for one who dares
To hope you will forgive . . . —" etcetera—

(To the Capuchin)

Father, this letter concerns you . . .

(To CHRISTIAN*)*

—and you.

Listen:

*(The others gather around her. She pretends to
read from the letter, aloud.)*

"Mademoiselle:

The Cardinal
Will have his way, although against your will;
That is why I am sending this to you
By a most holy man, intelligent,
Discreet. You will communicate to him
Our order to perform, here and at once
The rite of . . .

(Turns the page)

—Holy Matrimony. You
And Christian will be married privately
In your house. I have sent him to you. I know
You hesitate. Be resigned, nevertheless,
To the Cardinal's command, who sends herewith
His blessing. Be assured also of my own
Respect and high consideration—*signed,*
Your very humble and—etcetera—"

THE CAPUCHIN

A noble lord! I said so—never fear—
A worthy lord!—a very worthy lord!—

ROXANE

(To CHRISTIAN*)*

Am I a good reader of letters?

CHRISTIAN

(Motions toward the Capuchin.)

Careful!—

ROXANE

(In a tragic tone)

Oh, this is terrible!

THE CAPUCHIN

(Turns the light of his lantern on CYRANO*)*

You are to be—

CHRISTIAN

I am the bridegroom!

THE CAPUCHIN

(Turns his lantern upon CHRISTIAN*; then, as if
some suspicion crossed his mind, upon seeing the
young man so handsome.)*

Oh—why, *you* . . .

ROXANE

(Quickly)

Look here—

"Postscript: Give to the Convent in my name
One hundred and twenty pistoles"—

THE CAPUCHIN

Think of it!

A worthy lord—a worthy lord! . . .

(To ROXANE, *solemnly)*

Daughter, resign yourself!

ROXANE

(With an air of martyrdom)

I am resigned . . .

(While RAGUENEAU *opens the door for the Capuchin and* CHRISTIAN *invites him to enter, she
turns to* CYRANO.)*

De Guiche may come. Keep him out here with you
Do not let him—

CYRANO

I understand!

(To the Capuchin)

How long

Will you be?—

117

THE CAPUCHIN

Oh, a quarter of an hour.

CYRANO

(Hurrying them into the house.)

Hurry—I'll wait here—

ROXANE

(To CHRISTIAN*)*

Come!

(They go into the house.)

CYRANO

Now then, to make

His Grace delay that quarter of an hour . . .
I have it!—up here—

> *(He steps on the bench, and climbs up the wall toward the balcony. The theorbos begin to play a mournful melody.)*

Sad music— Ah, a man! . . .

(The music pauses on a sinister tremolo.)

Oh—very much a man!

> *(He sits astride of the railing and, drawing toward him a long branch of one of the trees which border the garden wall, he grasps it with both hands, ready to swing himself down.)*

So—not too high—

(He peers down at the ground.)

I must float gently through the atmosphere—

DE GUICHE

(Enters, masked, groping in the dark toward the house.)

Where is that cursed, bleating Capuchin?

CYRANO

What if he knows my voice?—the devil!—Tic-tac,
Bergerac—we unlock our Gascon tongue;
A good strong accent—

DE GUICHE

Here is the house—all dark—

Damn this mask!—

> *(As he is about to enter the house, CYRANO leaps from the balcony, still holding fast to the branch, which bends and swings him between DE GUICHE and the door; then he releases the branch and pretends to fall heavily as though from a height. He lands flatly on the ground, where he lies motionless, as if stunned. DE GUICHE leaps back.)*

118

What is that?
*(When he lifts his eyes, the branch has sprung
back into place. He can see nothing but the sky;
he does not understand.)*

Why ... where did this man

Fall from?

CYRANO

(Sits up, and speaks with a strong accent.)
—The moon!

DE GUICHE

You—

CYRANO

From the moon, the moon!

I fell out of the moon!

DE GUICHE

The fellow is mad—

CYRANO

(Dreamily)

Where am I?

DE GUICHE

Why—

CYRANO

What time is it? What place

Is this? What day? What season?

DE GUICHE

You—

CYRANO

I am stunned!

DE GUICHE

My dear sir—

CYRANO

Like a bomb—a bomb—I fell

From the moon!

DE GUICHE

Now, see here—

CYRANO

*(Rising to his feet, and speaking in a terrible
voice.)*

I say, the moon!

DE GUICHE

(Recoils)

Very well—if you say so—
(Aside)

Raving mad!—

CYRANO
(Advancing upon him.)
I am not speaking metaphorically!
DE GUICHE
Pardon.
CYRANO
A hundred years—an hour ago—
I really cannot say how long I fell—
I was in yonder shining sphere—
DE GUICHE
(Shrugs)

Quite so.

Please let me pass.
CYRANO
(Interposes himself.)
Where am I? Tell the truth—
I can bear it. In what quarter of the globe
Have I descended like a meteorite?
DE GUICHE
Morbleu!
CYRANO
I could not choose my place to fall—
The earth spun round so fast— Was it the Earth,
I wonder?—Or is this another world?
Another moon? Whither have I been drawn
By the dead weight of my posterior?
DE GUICHE
Sir. I repeat—
CYRANO
(With a sudden cry, which causes DE GUICHE *to recoil again.)*
His face! My God—black!
DE GUICHE
(Carries his hand to his mask.)

Oh!—

CYRANO
(Terrified)
Are you a native? Is this Africa?
DE GUICHE
—This mask!
CYRANO
(Somewhat reassured)
Are we in Venice? Genoa?
120

DE GUICHE

(Tries to pass him.)

A lady is waiting for me.

CYRANO

(Quite happy again)

So this is Paris!

DE GUICHE

(Smiling in spite of himself.)

This fool becomes amusing.

CYRANO

Ah! You smile?

DE GUICHE

I do. Kindly permit me—

CYRANO

(Delighted)

Dear old Paris—

Well, well!—

(Wholly at his ease, smiles, bows, arranges his dress.)

Excuse my appearance. I arrive
By the last thunderbolt—a trifle singed
As I came through the ether. These long journeys—
You know! There are so few conveniences!
My eyes are full of star-dust. On my spurs,
Some sort of fur . . . Planet's apparently . . .

(Plucks something from his sleeve.)

Look—on my doublet— That's a Comet's hair!

(He blows something from the back of his hand.)

Phoo!

DE GUICHE

(Grows angry.)

Monsieur—

CYRANO

(As DE GUICHE *is about to push past, thrusts his leg in the way.)*

Here's a tooth, stuck in my boot,
From the Great Bear. Trying to get away,
I tripped over the Scorpion and came down
Slap, into one scale of the Balances—
The pointer marks my weight this moment . . .

(Pointing upward.)

See?

*(*DE GUICHE *makes a sudden movement.* CYRANO *catches his arm.)*

121

Be careful! If you struck me on the nose,
It would drip milk!

DE GUICHE

Milk?

CYRANO

From the Milky Way!

DE GUICHE

Hell!

CYRANO

No, no—Heaven.
(Crossing his arms.)

Curious place up there—
Did you know Sirius wore a nightcap? True!
(Confidentially)
The Little Bear is still too young to bite.
(Laughing)
My foot caught in the Lyre, and broke a string.
(Proudly)
Well—when I write my book, and tell the tale
Of my adventures—all these little stars
That shake out of my cloak—I must save those
To use for asterisks!

DE GUICHE

That will do now—
I wish—

CYRANO

Yes, yes—I know—

DE GUICHE

Sir—

CYRANO

You desire
To learn from my own lips the character
Of the moon's surface—its inhabitants
If any—

DE GUICHE

(Loses patience and shouts.)
I desire no such thing! I—

CYRANO *(Rapidly)*
You wish to know by what mysterious means
I reached the moon?—well—confidentially—
It was a new invention of my own.

DE GUICHE *(Discouraged)*
Drunk too—as well as mad!

                                    I scorned the eagle
Of Regiomontanus, and the dove
Of Archytas!

DE GUICHE
                    A learned lunatic!—
CYRANO
I imitated no one. I myself
Discovered not one scheme merely, but six—
Six ways to violate the virgin sky!

> (DE GUICHE *has succeeded in passing him, and
> moves toward the door of* ROXANE'S *house.* CY-
> RANO *follows, ready to use violence if necessary.*)

DE GUICHE (*Looks around.*)
Six?

CYRANO
(With increasing volubility)
            As for instance—Having stripped myself
Bare as a wax candle, adorn my form
With crystal vials filled with morning dew,
And so be drawn aloft, as the sun rises
Drinking the mist of dawn!

DE GUICHE
(Takes a step toward CYRANO.)
                                    Yès—that makes one.

CYRANO
*(Draws back to lead him away from the door;
speaks faster and faster.)*
Or, sealing up the air in a cedar chest,
Rarefy it by means of mirrors, placed
In an icosahedron.

DE GUICHE
(Takes another step.)
                    Two.

CYRANO (*Still retreating*)
                            Again,
I might construct a rocket, in the form
Of a huge locust, driven by impulses
Of villainous saltpetre from the rear,
Upward, by leaps and bounds.

DE GUICHE
*(Interested in spite of himself, and counting on his
fingers.)*
                                    Three.

CYRANO *(Same business)*

Or again,

Smoke having a natural tendency to rise,
Blow in a globe enough to raise me.

DE GUICHE
(Same business, more and more astonished.)

Four!

CYRANO

Or since Diana, as old fables tell,
Draws forth to fill her crescent horn, the marrow
Of bulls and goats—to anoint myself therewith.

DE GUICHE
(Hypnotized)

Five!—

CYRANO
*(Has by this time led him all the way across the
street, close to a bench.)*
Finally—seated on an iron plate,
To hurl a magnet in the air—the iron
Follows—I catch the magnet—throw again—
And so proceed indefinitely.

DE GUICHE

Six!—

All excellent,—and which did you adopt?

CYRANO *(Coolly)*

Why, none of them. . . . A seventh.

DE GUICHE

Which was?—

CYRANO

Guess!—

DE GUICHE

An interesting idiot, this!

CYRANO
*(Imitates the sound of waves with his voice, and
their movement by large, vague gestures.)*

Hoo! . . . Hoo! . . .

DE GUICHE

Well?

CYRANO

Have you guessed it yet?

DE GUICHE

Why, no.

CYRANO
(Grandiloquent)

The ocean! . . .

124

What hour its rising tide seeks the full moon,
I laid me on the strand, fresh from the spray,
My head fronting the moonbeams, since the hair
Retains moisture—and so I slowly rose
As upon angels' wings, effortlessly,
Upward—then suddenly I felt a shock!—
And then . . .

DE GUICHE

> *(Overcome by curiosity, sits down on the bench.)*
> And then?

CYRANO

> And then—
> *(Changes abruptly to his natural voice.)*
> The time is up!—

Fifteen minutes, your Grace!—You are now free;
And—they are bound—in wedlock.

DE GUICHE

> *(Leaping up)*

Am *I* drunk?

That voice . . .

> *(The door of ROXANE's house opens; lackeys appear, bearing lighted candles. Lights up. CYRANO removes his hat.)*
> And that nose!—Cyrano!

CYRANO

> *(Saluting)*

Cyrano! . . .

This very moment, they have exchanged rings.

DE GUICHE

Who?

> *(He turns up stage. TABLEAU: between the lackeys, ROXANE and CHRISTIAN appear, hand in hand. The Capuchin follows them, smiling. RAGUENEAU holds aloft a torch. The Duenna brings up the rear, in a negligée, and a pleasant flutter of emotion.)*
> Zounds!
> *(To ROXANE)*
> You?—
> *(Recognizes CHRISTIAN)*
> He?—
> *(Saluting ROXANE)*

My sincere compliments!

> *(To CYRANO)*

You also, my inventor of machines!

125

Your rigmarole would have detained a saint
Entering Paradise—decidedly
You must not fail to write that book some day!

CYRANO

(Bowing)

Sir, I engage myself to do so.

> *(Leads the bridal pair down to* DE GUICHE *and
> strokes with great satisfaction his long white
> beard.)*

My lord,
The handsome couple you—and God—have joined
Together!

DE GUICHE

(Regarding him with a frosty eye.)
Quite so.
(Turns to ROXANE*)*

Madame, kindly bid
Your . . . husband farewell.

ROXANE

Oh!—

DE GUICHE

(To CHRISTIAN*)*

Your regiment
Leaves to-night, sir. Report at once!

ROXANE

You mean
For the front? The war?

DE GUICHE

Certainly!

ROXANE

I thought
The Cadets were not going—

DE GUICHE

Oh yes, they are!
(Taking out the despatch from his pocket.)
Here is the order—
(To CHRISTIAN*)*
Baron! Deliver this.

ROXANE

(Throws herself into CHRISTIAN'S *arms.)*
Christian!

DE GUICHE

(To CYRANO, *sneering)*
The bridal night is not so near!

CYRANO *(Aside)*
Somehow that news fails to disquiet me.

CHRISTIAN

(To ROXANE*)*
Your lips again . . .

CYRANO

There . . . That will do now— Come!

CHRISTIAN
(Still holding ROXANE*)*
You do not know how hard it is—

CYRANO
(Tries to drag him away.)

I know!
(The beating of drums is heard in the distance.)

DE GUICHE
(Up stage)
The regiment—on the march!

ROXANE
(As CYRANO *tries to lead* CHRISTIAN *away, follows,
and detains them.)*

Take care of him
For me—*(Appealingly)*

Promise me never to let him do
Anything dangerous!

CYRANO

I'll do my best—
I cannot promise—

ROXANE
(Same business)

Make him be careful!

CYRANO

Yes—
I'll try—

ROXANE
(Same business)
Be sure to keep him dry and warm!

CYRANO
Yes, yes—if possible—

ROXANE
(Same business; confidentially, in his ear)

See that he remains
Faithful!—

CYRANO
Of course! If—

127

ROXANE

(Same business)

And have him write to me
Every single day!

CYRANO *(Stops)*

That, I promise you!

(Curtain)

THE FOURTH ACT

THE CADETS OF GASCOYNE

THE POST *occupied by the Company of* CARBON DE CASTEL-JALOUX *at* THE SIEGE OF ARRAS.

In the background, a Rampart traversing the entire scene; beyond this, and apparently below, a Plain stretches away to the horizon. The country is cut up with earthworks and other suggestions of the siege. In the distance, against the sky-line, the houses and the walls of Arras.

Tents; scattered Weapons; Drums, et cetera. It is near daybreak, and the East is yellow with approaching dawn. Sentries at intervals. Camp-fires.

CURTAIN RISE *discovers the Cadets asleep, rolled in their cloaks.* CARBON DE CASTEL-JALOUX *and* LE BRET *keep watch. They are both very thin and pale.* CHRISTIAN *is asleep among the others, wrapped in his cloak, in the foreground, his face lighted by the flickering fire. Silence.*

LE BRET

Horrible!

CARBON
Why, yes. All of that.

LE BRET

Mordious!

CARBON
(Gesture toward the sleeping Cadets)
Swear gently— You might wake them.
(To Cadets)

Go to sleep—

Hush!

(To LE BRET*)*
Who sleeps dines.

LE BRET

I have insomnia.

God! What a famine.
(Firing off stage.)

129

CARBON

Curse that musketry!

They'll wake my babies.
(To the men)

Go to sleep!—

A CADET

(Rouses)

Diantre!

Again?

CARBON

No—only Cyrano coming home.
*(The heads which have been raised sink back
again.)*

A SENTRY

(Off stage)

Halt! Who goes there?

VOICE OF CYRANO

Bergerac!

THE SENTRY ON THE PARAPET

Halt! Who goes?—

CYRANO

(Appears on the parapet.)

Bergerac, idiot!

LE BRET

(Goes to meet him.)

Thank God again!

CYRANO

(Signs to him not to wake anyone.)

Hush!

LE BRET

Wounded?—

CYRANO

No— They always miss me—quite

A habit by this time!

LE BRET

Yes— Go right on—

Risk your life every morning before breakfast
To send a letter!

CYRANO

(Stops near CHRISTIAN.)

I promised he should write

Every single day . . .
(Looks down at him.)

Hm— The boy looks pale

When he is asleep—thin too—starving to death—
If that poor child knew! Handsome, none the less . . .

LE BRET

Go and get some sleep!

CYRANO

(Affectionately)

Now, now—you old bear,
No growling!—I am careful—you know I am—
Every night, when I cross the Spanish lines
I wait till they are all drunk.

LE BRET

You might bring
Something with you.

CYRANO

I have to travel light
To pass through— By the way, there will be news
For you to-day: the French will eat or die,
If what I saw means anything.

LE BRET

Tell us!

CYRANO

No—
I am not sure—we shall see!

CARBON

What a war,
When the besieger starves to death!

LE BRET

Fine war—
Fine situation! We besiege Arras—
The Cardinal Prince of Spain besieges us—
And—here we are!

CYRANO

Someone might besiege *him.*

CARBON

A hungry joke!

CYRANO

Ho, ho!

LE BRET

Yes, you can laugh—
Risking a life like yours to carry letters—
Where are you going now?

CYRANO

(At the tent door)

To write another.

(Goes into tent.)

(A little more daylight. The clouds redden. The town of Arras shows on the horizon. A cannon shot is heard, followed immediately by a roll of drums, far away to the left. Other drums beat a little nearer. The drums go on answering each other here and there, approach, beat loudly almost on the stage, and die away toward the right, across the camp. The camp awakes. Voices of officers in the distance.)

CARBON

(Sighs)

Those drums!—another good nourishing sleep
Gone to the devil.

(The Cadets rouse themselves.)

Now then!—

FIRST CADET

(Sits up, yawns.)

God! I'm hungry!

SECOND CADET

Starving!

ALL

(Groan)

Aoh!

CARBON

Up with you!

THIRD CADET

Not another step!

FOURTH CADET

Not another movement!

FIRST CADET

Look at my tongue—

I said this air was indigestible!

FIFTH CADET

My coronet for half a pound of cheese!

SIXTH CADET

I have no stomach for this war—I'll stay
In my tent—like Achilles.

ANOTHER

Yes—no bread,

No fighting—

CARBON

Cyrano!

OTHERS

May as well die—

132

Come out here!—You know how to talk to them.
Get them laughing—

SECOND CADET
*(Rushes up to First Cadet who is eating some-
thing.)*

What are you gnawing there?

FIRST CADET
Gun wads and axle-grease. Fat country this
Around Arras.

ANOTHER
(Enters)

I have been out hunting!

ANOTHER
(Enters)

Went fishing, in the Scarpe!

ALL
(Leaping up and surrounding the newcomers.)

Find anything?

Any fish? Any game? Perch? Partridges?
Let me look!

THE FISHERMAN
Yes—one gudgeon.

(Shows it.)

THE HUNTER
One fat . . . sparrow.

(Shows it.)

ALL
Ah!—See here, this—mutiny!—

CARBON
Cyrano!

Come and help!

CYRANO
(Enters from tent.)
Well?

*(Silence. To the First Cadet who is walking away,
with his chin on his chest.)*

You there, with the long face?

FIRST CADET
I have something on my mind that troubles me.

CYRANO
What is that?

FIRST CADET
My stomach.

133

CYRANO

So have I.

FIRST CADET

No doubt

You enjoy this!

CYRANO

(Tightens his belt.)

It keeps me looking young.

SECOND CADET

My teeth are growing rusty.

CYRANO

Sharpen them!

THIRD CADET

My belly sounds as hollow as a drum.

CYRANO

Beat the long roll on it!

FOURTH CADET

My ears are ringing.

CYRANO

Liar! A hungry belly has no ears.

FIFTH CADET

Oh for a barrel of good wine!

CYRANO

(Offers him his own helmet.)

Your casque.

SIXTH CADET

I'll swallow anything!

CYRANO

(Throws him the book which he has in his hand.)

Try the "Iliad."

SEVENTH CADET

The Cardinal, he has four meals a day—
What does he care!

CYRANO

Ask him; he really ought

To send you . . . a spring lamb out of his flock,
Roasted whole—

THE CADET

Yes, and a bottle—

CYRANO

*(Exaggerates the manner of one speaking to a
    servant.)*

If you please,

Richelieu—a little more of the Red Seal . . .
Ah, thank you!

And the salad—
CYRANO

Of course—Romaine!
ANOTHER CADET
(Shivering)
I am as hungry as a wolf.
CYRANO
(Tosses him a cloak.)

Put on

Your sheep's clothing.
FIRST CADET
(With a shrug)

Always the clever answer!
CYRANO
Always the answer—yes! Let me die so—
Under some rosy-golden sunset, saying
A good thing, for a good cause! By the sword,
The point of honor—by the hand of one
Worthy to be my foeman, let me fall—
Steel in my heart, and laughter on my lips!
VOICES HERE AND THERE
All very well— We are hungry!
CYRANO

Bah! You think
Of nothing but yourselves.
(His eye singles out the old fifer in the background.)

Here, Bertrandou,

You were a shepherd once— Your pipe now! Come,
Breathe, blow,— Play to these belly-worshippers
The old airs of the South—

"Airs with a smile in them,

Airs with a sigh in them, airs with the breeze
And the blue of the sky in them—"

Small, demure tunes

Whose every note is like a little sister—
Songs heard only in some long silent voice
Not quite forgotten— Mountain melodies
Like thin smoke rising from brown cottages
In the still noon, slowly— Quaint lullabies,
Whose very music has a Southern tongue—
(The old man sits down and prepares his fife.)
Now let the fife, that dry old warrior,
Dream, while over the stops your fingers dance

135

A minuet of little birds—let him
Dream beyond ebony and ivory;
Let him remember he was once a reed
Out of the river, and recall the spirit
Of innocent, untroubled country days . . .

> *(The fifer begins to play a Provençal melody.)*

Listen, you Gascons! Now it is no more
The shrill fife— It is the flute, through woodlands
    far
Away, calling—no longer the hot battle-cry,
But the cool, quiet pipe our goatherds play!
Listen—the forest glens . . . the hills . . . the downs . . .
The green sweetness of night on the Dordogne . . .
Listen, you Gascons! It is all Gascoyne! . . .

> *(Every head is bowed; every eye cast down. Here
> and there a tear is furtively brushed away with
> the back of a hand, the corner of a cloak.)*

CARBON

> *(Softly to* CYRANO)

You make them weep—

CYRANO

               For homesickness—a hunger
More noble than that hunger of the flesh;
It is their hearts now that are starving.

CARBON

                        Yes,
But you melt down their manhood.

CYRANO

> *(Motions the drummer to approach.)*

                       You think so?
Let them be. There is iron in their blood
Not easily dissolved in tears. You need
Only—

> *(He makes a gesture; the drum beats.)*

ALL

> *(Spring up and rush toward their weapons.)*

What's that? Where is it?—What?—

CYRANO

> *(Smiles)*

                       You see—
Let Mars snore in his sleep once—and farewell
Venus—sweet dreams—regrets—dear thoughts of home—
All the fife lulls to rest wakes at the drums!

A CADET

> *(Looks up stage.)*

Aha— Monsieur de Guiche!

(Mutter among themselves.)

Ugh! . . .

CYRANO

(Smiles)

Flattering
Murmur!

A CADET

He makes me weary!

ANOTHER

With his collar
Of lace over his corselet—

ANOTHER

Like a ribbon
Tied round a sword!

ANOTHER

Bandages for a boil
On the back of his neck—

SECOND CADET

A courtier always!

ANOTHER

The Cardinal's nephew!

CARBON

None the less—a Gascon.

FIRST CADET

A counterfeit! Never you trust that man—
Because we Gascons, look you, are all mad—
This fellow is reasonable—nothing more
Dangerous than a reasonable Gascon!

LE BRET

He looks pale.

ANOTHER

Oh, he can be hungry too,
Like any other poor devil—but he wears
So many jewels on that belt of his
That his cramps glitter in the sun!

CYRANO

(Quickly)

Is he
To see us looking miserable? Quick—
Pipes!—Cards!—Dice!—
*(They all hurriedly begin to play, on their stools, on
the drums, or on their cloaks spread on the
ground, lighting their long pipes meanwhile.)*

As for me, I read Descartes.

*(He walks up and down, reading a small book which
he takes from his pocket.* TABLEAU: DE GUICHE
*enters, looking pale and haggard. All are absorbed
in their games. General air of contentment.* DE
GUICHE *goes to* CARBON. *They look at each other
askance, each observing with satisfaction the con-
dition of the other.)*

DE GUICHE

Good morning!
(Aside)

He looks yellow.

CARBON
(Same business)

He is all eyes.

DE GUICHE
(Looks at the Cadets.)

What have we here? Black looks? Yes, gentlemen—
I am informed I am not popular;
The hill-nobility, barons of Béarn,
The pomp and pride of Périgord—I learn
They disapprove their colonel; call him courtier,
Politician—they take it ill that I
Cover my steel with lace of Genoa.
It is a great offense to be a Gascon
And not to be a beggar!
(Silence. They smoke. They play.)

Well—Shall I have

Your captain punish you? . . . No.

CARBON

As to that,

It would be impossible.

DE GUICHE
Oh?

CARBON

I am free;

I pay my company; it is my own;
I obey military orders.

DE GUICHE
Oh!

That will be quite enough.
(To the Cadets)

I can afford

Your little hates. My conduct under fire
Is well known. It was only yesterday
I drove the Count de Bucquoi from Bapaume,

Pouring my men down like an avalanche,
I myself led the charge—

CYRANO

(Without looking up from his book.)

And your white scarf?

DE GUICHE

(Surprised and gratified)

You heard that episode? Yes—rallying
My men for the third time, I found myself
Carried among a crowd of fugitives
Into the enemy's lines. I was in danger
Of being shot or captured; but I thought
Quickly—took off and flung away the scarf
That marked my military rank—and so
Being inconspicuous, escaped among
My own force, rallied them, returned again
And won the day! . . .

*(The Cadets do not appear to be listening, but here
and there the cards and the dice boxes remain
motionless, the smoke is retained in their cheeks.)*

What do you say to that?

Presence of mind—yes?

CYRANO

Henry of Navarre

Being outnumbered, never flung away
His white plume.

*(Silent enjoyment. The cards flutter, the dice roll,
the smoke puffs out.)*

DE GUICHE

My device was a success,

However!

*(Same attentive pause, interrupting the games and
the smoking.)*

CYRANO

Possibly . . . An officer

Does not lightly resign the privilege
Of being a target.

*(Cards, dice, and smoke fall, roll, and float away
with increasing satisfaction.)*

Now, if I had been there—

Your courage and my own differ in this—
When your scarf fell, I should have put it on.

DE GUICHE

Boasting again!

CYRANO

Boasting? Lend it to me
To-night; I'll lead the first charge, with your scarf
Over my shoulder!

DE GUICHE

Gasconnade once more!
You are safe making that offer, and you know it—
My scarf lies on the river bank between
The lines, a spot swept by artillery
Impossible to reach alive!

CYRANO

(Produces the scarf from his pocket.)
Yes. Here . . .

*(Silence. The Cadets stifle their laughter behind
their cards and their dice boxes.* DE GUICHE
*turns to look at them. Immediately they resume
their gravity and their game. One of them
whistles carelessly the mountain air which the
fifer was playing.)*

DE GUICHE

(Takes the scarf.)
Thank you! That bit of white is what I need
To make a signal. I was hesitating—
You have decided me.

*(He goes up to the parapet, climbs upon it, and
waves the scarf at arm's length several times.)*

ALL

What is he doing?—

What?—

THE SENTRY ON THE PARAPET

There's a man down there running away!

DE GUICHE

(Descending)
A Spaniard. Very useful as a spy
To both sides. He informs the enemy
As I instruct him. By his influence
I can arrange their dispositions.

CYRANO

Traitor!

DE GUICHE

(Folding the scarf.)
A traitor, yes; but useful . . .

We were saying? . . .

Oh, yes— Here is a bit of news for you:
Last night we had hopes of reprovisioning

The army. Under cover of the dark,
The Marshal moved to Dourlens. Our supplies
Are there. He may reach them. But to return
Safely, he needs a large force—at least half
Our entire strength. At present, we have here
Merely a skeleton.

CARBON

Fortunately,
The Spaniards do not know that.

DE GUICHE

Oh, yes; they know

They will attack.

CARBON

Ah!

DE GUICHE

From that spy of mine
I learned of their intention. His report
Will determine the point of their advance.
The fellow asked me what to say! I told him:
"Go out between the lines; watch for my signal;
Where you see that, let them attack there."

CARBON

(To the Cadets)

Well,

Gentlemen!

(All rise. Noise of sword belts and breastplates being buckled on.)

DE GUICHE

You may have perhaps an hour.

FIRST CADET

Oh— An hour!

(They all sit down and resume their games once more.)

DE GUICHE

(To CARBON)

The great thing is to gain time.
Any moment the Marshal may return.

CARBON

And to gain time?

DE GUICHE

You will all be so kind
As to lay down your lives!

CYRANO

Ah! Your revenge?

141

I make no great pretence of loving you!
But—since you gentlemen esteem yourselves
Invincible, the bravest of the brave,
And all that—why need we be personal?
I serve the king in choosing . . . as I choose!

CYRANO

(Salutes)

Sir, permit me to offer—all our thanks.

DE GUICHE

(Returns the salute.)

You love to fight a hundred against one;
Here is your opportunity!

(He goes up stage with CARBON.*)*

CYRANO

(To the Cadets)

My friends,

We shall add now to our old Gascon arms
With their six chevrons, blue and gold, a seventh—
Blood-red!

*(*DE GUICHE *talks in a low tone to* CARBON *up
stage. Orders are given. The defense is arranged.*
CYRANO *goes to* CHRISTIAN *who has remained
motionless with folded arms.)*

Christian?

(Lays a hand on his shoulder.)

CHRISTIAN

(Shakes his head.)

Roxane . . .

CYRANO

Yes.

CHRISTIAN

I should like

To say farewell to her, with my whole heart
Written for her to keep.

CYRANO

I thought of that—

(Takes a letter from his doublet.)

I have written your farewell.

CHRISTIAN

Show me!

CYRANO

You wish

To read it?

142

CHRISTIAN
    Of course!
    (He takes the letter; begins to read, looks up suddenly.)

                What?—
CYRANO
                            What is it?

CHRISTIAN
                                Look—
This little circle—
CYRANO
    (Takes back the letter quickly, and looks innocent.)
                Circle?—
CHRISTIAN
                    Yes—a tear!
CYRANO
So it is! . . . Well—a poet while he writes
Is like a lover in his lady's arms,
Believing his imagination—all
Seems true—you understand? There's half the charm
Of writing— Now, this letter as you see
I have made so pathetic that I wept
While I was writing it!

CHRISTIAN
            You—wept?
CYRANO
                            Why, yes—
Because . . . it is a little thing to die,
But—not to see her . . . that is terrible!
And I shall never—
            (CHRISTIAN looks at him.)
                    We shall never—
    (Quickly)
                            You
Will never—
CHRISTIAN
    (Snatches the letter.)
        Give me that!
    (Noise in the distance on the outskirts of the camp)
    VOICE OF A SENTRY
                    Halt—who goes there?
    (Shots, shouting, jingle of harness)
        CARBON
What is it?—

143

Why, a coach.
(They rush to look.)
CONFUSED VOICES

What? In the Camp?

A coach? Coming this way— It must have driven
Through the Spanish lines—what the devil— Fire!—
No— Hark! The driver shouting—what does he say?
Wait— He said: "On the service of the King!"
*(They are all on the parapet looking over. The
jingling comes nearer.)*
DE GUICHE
Of the King?
(They come down and fall into line.)
CARBON
Hats off, all!
DE GUICHE
(Speaks off stage.)

The King! Fall in,

Rascals!—
*(The coach enters at full trot. It is covered with
mud and dust. The curtains are drawn. Two foot-
men are seated behind. It stops suddenly.)*
CARBON
(Shouts)
Beat the assembly—
(Roll of drums. All the Cadets uncover.)
DE GUICHE

Two of you,

Lower the steps—open the door—
(Two men rush to the coach. The door opens.)
ROXANE
(Comes out of the coach.)

Good morning!

*(At the sound of a woman's voice, every head is
raised. Sensation.)*
DE GUICHE
On the King's service— You?
ROXANE

Yes—my own king—

Love!
CYRANO
(Aside)
God is merciful . . .

144

CHRISTIAN

(Hastens to her.)

You! Why have you—

ROXANE

Your war lasted so long!

CHRISTIAN

But why?—

ROXANE

Not now—

CYRANO

(Aside)

I wonder if I dare to look at her . . .

DE GUICHE

You cannot remain here!

ROXANE

Why, certainly!

Roll that drum here, somebody . . .

(She sits on the drum, which is brought to her.)

Thank you— There!

(She laughs.)

Would you believe—they fired upon us?

—My coach

Looks like the pumpkin in the fairy tale,
Does it not? And my footmen—

(She throws a kiss to CHRISTIAN.)

How do you do?

(She looks about.)

How serious you all are! Do you know,
It is a long drive here—from Arras?

(Sees CYRANO.)

Cousin,

I am glad to see you!

CYRANO

(Advances)

Oh— How did you come?

ROXANE

How did I find you? Very easily—
I followed where the country was laid waste
—Oh, but I saw such things! I had to see
To believe. Gentlemen, is that the service
Of your King? I prefer my own!

CYRANO

But how

Did you come through?

145

ROXANE

             Why, through the Spanish lines

Of course!

FIRST CADET

    They let you pass?—

DE GUICHE

                 What did you say?

How did you manage?

LE BRET

             Yes, that must have been

Difficult!

ROXANE

    No— I simply drove along.
Now and then some hidalgo scowled at me
And I smiled back—my best smile; whereupon,
The Spaniards being (without prejudice
To the French) the most polished gentlemen
In the world—I passed!

CARBON

             Certainly that smile
Should be a passport! Did they never ask
Your errand or your destination?

ROXANE

                 Oh,

Frequently! Then I dropped my eyes and said:
"I have a lover . . ." Whereupon, the Spaniard
With an air of ferocious dignity
Would close the carriage door—with such a gesture
As any king might envy, wave aside
The muskets that were levelled at my breast,
Fall back three paces, equally superb
In grace and gloom, draw himself up, thrust forth
A spur under his cloak, sweeping the air
With his long plumes, bow very low, and say:
"Pass, Señorita!"

CHRISTIAN

    But Roxane—

ROXANE

               I know—

I said "a lover"—but you understand—
Forgive me!—If I said "I am going to meet
My husband," no one would believe me!

CHRISTIAN

               Yes,

But—

ROXANE

What then?

DE GUICHE

You must leave this place.

CYRANO

At once.

ROXANE

I?

LE BRET

Yes—immediately.

ROXANE

And why?

CHRISTIAN

(Embarrassed)

Because . . .

CYRANO

(Same)

In half an hour . . .

DE GUICHE

(Same)

Or these quarters . . .

CARBON

(Same)

Perhaps

It might be better . . .

LE BRET

If you . . .

ROXANE

Oh— I see!

You are going to fight. I remain here.

ALL

No—no!

ROXANE

He is my husband—

(Throws herself in CHRISTIAN'S *arms.)*

I will die with you!

CHRISTIAN

Your eyes! . . . Why do you?—

ROXANE

You know why . . .

DE GUICHE

(Desperate)

This post

Is dangerous—

ROXANE

(Turns)

How—dangerous?

CYRANO

The proof
Is, we are ordered—

ROXANE

(To DE GUICHE*)*

Oh—you wish to make
A widow of me?

DE GUICHE

On my word of honor—

ROXANE

No matter. I am just a little mad—
I will stay. It may be amusing.

CYRANO

What,
A heroine—our intellectual?

ROXANE

Monsieur de Bergerac, I am your cousin!

A CADET

We'll fight now! Hurrah!

ROXANE

(More and more excited)

I am safe with you—my friends!

ANOTHER

(Carried away)

The whole camp breathes of lilies!—

ROXANE

And I think,
This hat would look well on the battlefield! . . .
But perhaps—

(Looks at DE GUICHE.*)*

The Count ought to leave us. Any moment
Now, there may be danger.

DE GUICHE

This is too much!
I must inspect my guns. I shall return—
You may change your mind— There will yet be
    time—

ROXANE

Never!

*(*DE GUICHE *goes out.)*

CHRISTIAN

(Imploring)
Roxane! . . .

ROXANE

No!

FIRST CADET

(To the rest)

She stays here!

ALL

(Rushing about, elbowing each other, brushing off their clothes.)

A comb!—

Soap!—Here's a hole in my— A needle!—Who
Has a ribbon?—Your mirror, quick!—My cuffs—
A razor—

ROXANE

(To CYRANO, *who is still urging her)*
No! I shall not stir one step!

CARBON

(Having, like the others, tightened his belt, dusted himself, brushed off his hat, smoothed out his plume and put on his lace cuffs, advances to ROXANE *ceremoniously.)*

In that case, may I not present to you
Some of these gentlemen who are to have
The honor of dying in your presence?

ROXANE

(Bows)

Please!—

(She waits, standing, on the arm of CHRISTIAN, *while*

CARBON

—*presents)*

Baron de Peyrescous de Colignac!

THE CADET

(Salutes)

Madame . . .

ROXANE

Monsieur . . .

CARBON

(Continues)

Baron de Casterac
De Cahuzac—Vidame de Malgouyre
Estressac Lésbas d'Escarabiot—

149

THE VIDAME

Madame . . .

CARBON

Chevalier d'Antignac-Juzet—
Baron Hillot de Blagnac-Saléchan
De Castel-Crabioules—

THE BARON

Madame . . .

ROXANE

How many

Names you all have!

THE BARON

Hundreds!

CARBON

(To ROXANE*)*

Open the hand

That holds your handkerchief.

ROXANE

(Opens her hand; the handkerchief falls.)

Why?

(The whole company makes a movement toward it.)

CARBON

(Picks it up quickly.)

My company

Was in want of a banner. We have now
The fairest in the army!

ROXANE

(Smiling)

Rather small—

CARBON

(Fastens the handkerchief to his lance.)

Lace—and embroidered!

A CADET

(To the others)

With her smiling on me,

I could die happy, if I only had
Something in my—

CARBON

(Turns upon him)

Shame on you! Feast your eyes

And forget your—

ROXANE

(Quickly)

It must be this fresh air—

I am starving! Let me see . . .

Cold partridges,
Pastry, a little white wine—that would do.
Will some one bring that to me?

THE CADET

(Aside)

Will some one !—

ANOTHER

Where the devil are we to find—

ROXANE

(Overhears; sweetly)

Why, there—

In my carriage.

ALL

Wha-at?

ROXANE

All you have to do
Is to unpack, and carve, and serve things.

Oh,

Notice my coachman; you may recognize
An old friend.

THE CADETS

(Rush to the coach.)

Ragueneau !

ROXANE

(Follows them with her eyes.)

Poor fellows . . .

THE CADETS

(Acclamations)

Ah !

Ah !

CYRANO

(Kisses her hand.)

Our good fairy !

RAGUENEAU

(Standing on his box, like a mountebank before a crowd.)

Gentlemen !—

(Enthusiasm)

THE CADETS

Bravo !

Bravo !

RAGUENEAU

The Spaniards, basking in our smiles,
Smiled on our baskets !

(Applause)

151

CYRANO
(Aside, to CHRISTIAN)

Christian!—

RAGUENEAU

They adored

The Fair, and missed—
(He takes from under the seat a dish, which he holds aloft.)
the Fowl!
(Applause. The dish is passed from hand to hand.)
CYRANO
(As before, to CHRISTIAN)

One moment—

RAGUENEAU

Venus

Charmed their eyes, while Adonis quietly
(Brandishing a ham.)
Brought home the Boar!
(Applause; the ham is seized by a score of hands outstretched.)
CYRANO
(As before)

Pst— Let me speak to you—
ROXANE
(As the Cadets return, their arms full of provisions)
Spread them out on the ground.
(Calls)

Christian! Come here;
Make yourself useful.
*(*CHRISTIAN *turns to her, at the moment when* CYRANO *was leading him aside. She arranges the food, with his aid and that of the two imperturbable footmen.)*
RAGUENEAU
Peacock, aux truffes!
FIRST CADET
(Comes down, cutting a huge slice of the ham.)
Tonnerre!
We are not going to die without a gorge—
(Sees ROXANE; *corrects himself hastily.)*
Pardon—a banquet!
RAGUENEAU
(Tossing out the cushions of the carriage.)
Open these—they are full

Of ortolans!
> *(Tumult; laughter; the cushions are eviscerated.)*
>> THIRD CADET
>> Lucullus!
>>> RAGUENEAU
>>> *(Throws out bottles of red wine.)*
>>>> Flasks of ruby—
> *(And of white)*
Flasks of topaz—
>> ROXANE
>> *(Throws a tablecloth at the head of CYRANO.)*
>>> Come back out of your dreams!
Unfold this cloth—
>> RAGUENEAU
>> *(Takes off one of the lanterns of the carriage, and*
>> *flourishes it.)*
>>> Our lamps are bonbonnières!
>>> CYRANO
>>> *(To CHRISTIAN)*
I must see you before you speak with her—
>> RAGUENEAU
>> *(More and more lyrical)*
My whip-handle is one long sausage!
>>> ROXANE
>>> *(Pouring wine; passing the food.)*
>>>> We
Being about to die, first let us dine!
Never mind the others—all for Gascoyne!
And if De Guiche comes, he is not invited!
> *(Going from one to another.)*
Plenty of time—you need not eat so fast—
Hold your cup—
> *(To another)*
>> What's the matter?
>>> THE CADET
>>> *(Sobbing)*
>>>> You are so good
To us . . .
>> ROXANE
>> There, there! Red or white wine?
>>> —Some bread
For Monsieur de Carbon!—Napkins— A knife—
Pass your plate— Some of the crust? A little more—
Light or dark?—Burgundy?—

153

CYRANO

*(Follows her with an armful of dishes, helping to
serve.)*

Adorable!

ROXANE

(Goes to CHRISTIAN.*)*

What would you like?

CHRISTIAN

Nothing.

ROXANE

Oh, but you must!—

A little wine? A biscuit?

CHRISTIAN

Tell me first

Why you came—

ROXANE

By and by. I must take care

Of these poor boys—

LE BRET

*(Who has gone up stage to pass up food to the
sentry on the parapet, on the end of a lance.)*

De Guiche!—

CYRANO

Hide everything

Quick!—Dishes, bottles, tablecloth—

Now look

Hungry again—

(To RAGUENEAU*)*

You there! Up on your box—

—Everything out of sight?—

*(In a twinkling, everything has been pushed inside
the tents, hidden in their hats or under their
cloaks.* DE GUICHE *enters quickly, then stops,
sniffing the air. Silence.)*

DE GUICHE

It smells good here.

A CADET

(Humming with an air of great unconcern.)

Sing ha-ha-ha and ho-ho-ho—

DE GUICHE

(Stares at him; he grows embarrassed.)

You there—

What are you blushing for?

154

THE CADET

Nothing—my blood
Stirs at the thought of battle.

ANOTHER

Pom ... pom ... pom ! ...

DE GUICHE
(Turns upon him.)
What is that?

THE CADET
(Slightly stimulated)
Only song—only little song—

DE GUICHE
You appear happy !

THE CADET

Oh yes—always happy
Before a fight—

DE GUICHE
(Calls to CARBON, for the purpose of giving him an order.)
Captain ! I—
(Stops and looks at him.)

What the devil—
You are looking happy too !—

CARBON
(Pulls a long face and hides a bottle behind his back.)
No !

DE GUICHE

Here—I had
One gun remaining. I have had it placed
(He points off stage.)
There—in that corner—for your men.

A CADET
(Simpering)

So kind !—
Charming attention !

ANOTHER
(Same business; burlesque)
Sweet solicitude !—

DE GUICHE
(Contemptuous)
I believe you are both drunk—
(Coldly)

Being unaccustomed

To guns—take care of the recoil!

FIRST CADET

(Gesture)

Ah-h . . . Pfft!

DE GUICHE

(Goes up to him, furious.)

How dare you?

FIRST CADET

A Gascon's gun never recoils!

DE GUICHE

(Shakes him by the arm.)

You *are* drunk—

FIRST CADET

(Superbly)

With the smell of powder!

DE GUICHE

(Turns away with a shrug.)

Bah!

(To ROXANE*)*

Madame, have you decided?

ROXANE

I stay here.

DE GUICHE

You have time to escape—

ROXANE

No!

DE GUICHE

Very well—

Someone give me a musket!

CARBON

What?

DE GUICHE

I stay

Here also.

CYRANO

(Formally)

Sir, you show courage!

FIRST CADET

A Gascon

In spite of all that lace!

ROXANE

Why—

DE GUICHE

Must I run

Away, and leave a woman?

156

SECOND CADET
(To First Cadet)

We might give him

Something to eat—what do you say?
(All the food re-appears, as if by magic.)

DE GUICHE
(His face lights up.)

A feast!

THIRD CADET

Here a little, there a little—

DE GUICHE
(Recovers his self-control; haughtily.)

Do you think

I want your leavings?

CYRANO
(Saluting)

Colonel—you improve!

DE GUICHE

I can fight as I am!

FIRST CADET
(Delighted)

Listen to him—

He has an accent!

DE GUICHE
(Laughs)

Have I so?

FIRST CADET

A Gascon!—

A Gascon, after all!
(They all begin to dance.)

CARBON
(Who has disappeared for a moment behind the parapet, reappears on top of it.)

I have placed my pikemen

Here.

(Indicates a row of pikes showing above the parapet.)

DE GUICHE
(Bows to ROXANE.*)*

We'll review them; will you take my arm?
(She takes his arm; they go up on the parapet. The rest uncover, and follow them up stage.)

CHRISTIAN
(Goes hurriedly to CYRANO.*)*

Speak quickly!

(At the moment when ROXANE *appears on the parapet the pikes are lowered in salute, and a cheer is heard. She bows.)*

THE PIKEMEN

(Off stage)

Hurrah!

CHRISTIAN

What is it?

CYRANO

If Roxane . . .

CHRISTIAN

Well?

CYRANO

Speaks about your letters . . .

CHRISTIAN

Yes—I know!

CYRANO

Do not make the mistake of showing . . .

CHRISTIAN

What?

CYRANO

Showing surprise.

CHRISTIAN

Surprise—why?

CYRANO

I must tell you! . . .

It is quite simple—I had forgotten it
Until just now. You have . . .

CHRISTIAN

Speak quickly!—

CYRANO

You

Have written oftener than you think.

CHRISTIAN

Oh—have I!

CYRANO

I took upon me to interpret you;
And wrote—sometimes . . . without . . .

CHRISTIAN

My knowing. Well?

CYRANO

Perfectly simple!

CHRISTIAN

Oh yes, perfectly!—

For a month, we have been blockaded here!—
How did you send all these letters?

CYRANO

Before
Daylight, I managed—

CHRISTIAN

I see. That was also
Perfectly simple!

—So I wrote to her,
How many times a week? Twice? Three times?
Four?

CYRANO

Oftener.

CHRISTIAN

Every day?

CYRANO

Yes—every day . . .
Every single day . . .

CHRISTIAN

(Violently)

And that wrought you up
Into such a flame that you faced death—

CYRANO

(Sees ROXANE returning.)

Hush—
Not before her!

*(He goes quickly into the tent. ROXANE comes up
to CHRISTIAN.)*

ROXANE

Now—Christian!

CHRISTIAN

(Takes her hands.)

Tell me now
Why you came here—over these ruined roads—
Why you made your way among mosstroopers
And ruffians—you—to join me here?

ROXANE

Because—
Your letters . . .

CHRISTIAN

Meaning?

ROXANE

It was your own fault
If I ran into danger! I went mad—

159

Mad with you! Think what you have written me,
How many times, each one more wonderful
Than the last!

CHRISTIAN
                    All this for a few absurd
Love-letters—

ROXANE
                    Hush—absurd! How can you know?
I thought I loved you, ever since one night
When a voice that I never would have known
Under my window breathed your soul to me . . .
But—all this time, your letters—every one
Was like hearing your voice there in the dark,
All around me, like your arms around me . . .
        (More lightly)

                                                At last,

I came. Anyone would! Do you suppose
The prim Penelope had stayed at home
Embroidering,—if Ulysses wrote like you?
She would have fallen like another Helen—
Tucked up those linen petticoats of hers
And followed him to Troy!

CHRISTIAN
                            But you—

ROXANE
                                    I read them

Over and over. I grew faint reading them.
I belonged to you. Every page of them
Was like a petal fallen from your soul—
Like the light and the fire of a great love,
Sweet and strong and true—

CHRISTIAN
                Sweet . . . and strong . . . and true . . .
You felt that, Roxane?—

ROXANE
                        You know how I feel! . . .

CHRISTIAN
So—you came . . .

ROXANE
                Oh, my Christian, oh my king,—
Lift me up if I fall upon my knees—
It is the heart of me that kneels to you,
And will remain forever at your feet—
You cannot lift that!—

                                I came here to say
'Forgive me'—(It is time to be forgiven
Now, when we may die presently)—forgive me
For being light and vain and loving you
Only because you were beautiful.

CHRISTIAN
(Astonished)

                                        Roxane! . . .

ROXANE

Afterwards I knew better. Afterwards
(I had to learn to use my wings) I loved you
For yourself too—knowing you more, and loving
More of you. And now—

CHRISTIAN
Now? . . .

ROXANE

                                        It is yourself

I love now: your own self.

CHRISTIAN
(Taken aback)

                                Roxane!

ROXANE
(Gravely)

                                        Be happy!—

You must have suffered; for you must have seen
How frivolous I was; and to be loved
For the mere costume, the poor casual body
You went about in—to a soul like yours,
That must have been torture! Therefore with words
You revealed your heart. Now that image of you
Which filled my eyes first—I see better now,
And I see it no more!

CHRISTIAN
Oh!—

ROXANE

                                You still doubt

Your victory?

CHRISTIAN
(Miserably)
Roxane!—

ROXANE

                                I understand:

You cannot perfectly believe in me—
A love like this—

161

CHRISTIAN

I want no love like this!
I want love only for—

ROXANE

Only for what
Every woman sees in you? I can do
Better than that!

CHRISTIAN

No—it was best before!

ROXANE

You do not altogether know me . . . Dear,
There is more of me than there was—with this,
I can love more of you—more of what makes
You your own self—Truly! . . . If you were less
Lovable—

CHRISTIAN

No!

ROXANE

—Less charming—ugly even—
I should love you still.

CHRISTIAN

You mean that?

ROXANE

I do
Mean that!

CHRISTIAN

Ugly? . . .

ROXANE

Yes. Even then!

CHRISTIAN

(Agonized)

Oh . . . God! . . .

ROXANE

Now are you happy?

CHRISTIAN

(Choking)

Yes . . .

ROXANE

What is it?

CHRISTIAN

(Pushes her away gently.)

Only . . .
Nothing . . . one moment . . .

ROXANE

But—

CHRISTIAN
(Gesture toward the Cadets)

I am keeping you
From those poor fellows— Go and smile at them;
They are going to die!

ROXANE
(Softly)

Dear Christian!

CHRISTIAN

Go—

(She goes up among the Gascons who gather round her respectfully.)

Cyrano!

CYRANO
(Comes out of the tent, armed for the battle.)
What is wrong? You look—

CHRISTIAN

She does not
Love me any more.

CYRANO
(Smiles)

You think not?

CHRISTIAN

She loves
You.

CYRANO

No!—

CHRISTIAN
(Bitterly)

She loves only my soul.

CYRANO

No!

CHRISTIAN

Yes—
That means you. And you love her.

CYRANO

I?

CHRISTIAN

I see—
I know!

CYRANO
That is true . . .

CHRISTIAN

More than—

163

CYRANO

(Quietly)

More than that.

CHRISTIAN

Tell her so!

CYRANO

No.

CHRISTIAN

Why not?

CYRANO

Why—look at me!

CHRISTIAN

She would love me if I were ugly.

CYRANO

(Startled)

She—

Said that?

CHRISTIAN

Yes. Now then!

CYRANO

(Half to himself)

It was good of her

To tell you that . . .
(Change of tone)

Nonsense! Do you believe

Any such madness—

It was good of her

To tell you. . . .

Do not take her at her word!

Go on—you never will be ugly— Go!

She would never forgive me.

CHRISTIAN

That is what

We shall see.

CYRANO

No, no—

CHRISTIAN

Let her choose between us!—

Tell her everything!

CYRANO

No—you torture me—

CHRISTIAN

Shall I ruin your happiness, because

I have a cursed pretty face? That seems

Too unfair!

CYRANO

And am I to ruin yours
Because I happen to be born with power
To say what you—perhaps—feel?

CHRISTIAN

Tell her!

CYRANO

Man—

Do not try me too far!

CHRISTIAN

I am tired of being

My own rival!

CYRANO

Christian!—

CHRISTIAN

Our secret marriage—

No witnesses—fraudulent—that can be
Annulled—

CYRANO

Do not try me—

CHRISTIAN

I want her love

For the poor fool I am—or not at all!
Oh, I am going through with this! I'll know,
One way or the other. Now I shall walk down
To the end of the post. Go tell her. Let her choose
One of us.

CYRANO

It will be you.

CHRISTIAN

God—I hope so!

(He turns and calls.)

Roxane!

CYRANO

No—no—

ROXANE
(Hurries down to him.)

Yes, Christian?

CHRISTIAN

Cyrano

Has news for you—important.

(She turns to CYRANO. CHRISTIAN *goes out.)*

ROXANE

(Lightly)

Oh—important?

CYRANO

He is gone . . .
    (To ROXANE)
                      Nothing—only Christian thinks
You ought to know—

ROXANE

                          I do know. He still doubts
What I told him just now. I saw that.

CYRANO

(Takes her hand.)
                                  Was it
True—what you told him just now?

ROXANE

                             It was true!
I said that I should love him even . . .

CYRANO

(Smiling sadly)
                              The word
Comes hard—before me?

ROXANE

                        Even if he were . . .

CYRANO

                                Say it—
I shall not be hurt!—Ugly?

ROXANE

                     Even then
I should love him.
    (A few shots, off stage, in the direction in which
      CHRISTIAN *disappeared.)*
                 Hark! The guns—

CYRANO

                          Hideous?

ROXANE

Hideous.

CYRANO

        Disfigured?

ROXANE

        Or disfigured.

CYRANO

                          Even
Grotesque?

ROXANE

      How could he ever be grotesque—
Ever—to me!

CYRANO

But you could love him so,

As much as?—

ROXANE

Yes—and more!

CYRANO

(Aside, excitedly)

It is true!—true!—

Perhaps—God! This is too much happiness . . .

(To ROXANE*)*

I—Roxane—listen—

LE BRET

(Enters quickly; calls to CYRANO *in a low tone.)*

Cyrano—

CYRANO

(Turns)

Yes?

LE BRET

Hush! . . .

(Whispers a few words to him.)

CYRANO

(Lets fall ROXANE'S *hand.)*

Ah!

ROXANE

What is it?

CYRANO

(Half stunned, and aside)

All gone . . .

ROXANE *(More shots)*

What is it? Oh,

They are fighting!—

(She goes up to look off stage.)

CYRANO

All gone. I cannot ever

Tell her, now . . . ever . . .

ROXANE

(Starts to rush away.)

What has happened?

CYRANO

(Restrains her.)

Nothing.

(Several Cadets enter. They conceal something which they are carrying, and form a group so as to prevent ROXANE *from seeing their burden.)*

167

ROXANE

These men—

CYRANO

Come away . . .
(He leads her away from the group.)

ROXANE

You were telling me

Something—

CYRANO

Oh, that? Nothing. . . . *(Gravely)*

I swear to you

That the spirit of Christian—that his soul
Was—

(Corrects himself quickly.)
That his soul is no less great—

ROXANE

(Catches at the word.)

Was?

(Crying out)

Oh!—
(She rushes among the men, and scatters them.)

CYRANO

All gone . . .

ROXANE

(Sees CHRISTIAN *lying upon his cloak.)*
Christian!

LE BRET *(To* CYRANO*)*

At the first volley.

*(*ROXANE *throws herself upon the body of* CHRIS-
TIAN. *Shots; at first scattered, then increasing.
Drums. Voices shouting.)*

CARBON

(Sword in hand)

Here

They come!—Ready!—
*(Followed by the Cadets, he climbs over the parapet
and disappears.)*

ROXANE

Christian!

CARBON *(Off stage)*

Come on, there, You!

ROXANE

Christian!

CARBON

Fall in!

168

ROXANE

Christian!

CARBON

Measure your fuse!

(RAGUENEAU *hurries up, carrying a helmet full of water.*)

CHRISTIAN *(Faintly)*

Roxane! . . .

CYRANO

(Low and quick, in CHRISTIAN'S *ear, while* ROXANE *is dipping into the water a strip of linen torn from her dress.)*

I have told her; she loves you.

(CHRISTIAN *closes his eyes.*)

ROXANE

(Turns to CHRISTIAN.*)*

Yes,

My darling?

CARBON

Draw your ramrods!

ROXANE *(To* CYRANO*)*

He is not dead? . . .

CARBON

Open your charges!

ROXANE

I can feel his cheek

Growing cold against mine—

CARBON

Take aim!

ROXANE

A letter—

Over his heart— *(She opens it.)*

For me.

CYRANO

(Aside)

My letter . . .

CARBON

Fire!

(Musketry, cries and groans. Din of battle.)

CYRANO

(Trying to withdraw his hand, which ROXANE, *still upon her knees, is holding.)*

But Roxane—they are fighting—

ROXANE

Wait a little . . .

He is dead. No one else knew him but you . . .
>   (*She weeps quietly.*)
Was he not a great lover, a great man,
A hero?

>   CYRANO
>   (*Standing, bareheaded.*)
>   Yes, Roxane.

>   ROXANE

>   A poet, unknown,

Adorable?

>   CYRANO
>   Yes, Roxane.

>   ROXANE

>   A fine mind?

>   CYRANO

Yes, Roxane.

>   ROXANE
>   A heart deeper than we knew—
A soul magnificently tender?
>   CYRANO (*Firmly*)

>   Yes,

Roxane!

>   ROXANE
>   (*Sinks down upon the breast of* CHRISTIAN.)
>   He is dead now . . .
>   CYRANO
>   (*Aside; draws his sword.*)

>   Why, so am I—
For I am dead, and my love mourns for me
And does not know . . . (*Trumpets in distance*)
>   DE GUICHE
>   (*Appears on the parapet, disheveled, wounded on
>   the forehead, shouting.*)
>   The signal—hark—the trumpets!
The army has returned— Hold them now!—Hold them!
The army!—

>   ROXANE
>   On his letter—blood . . . and tears.
>   A VOICE (*Off stage*)

Surrender!

>   THE CADETS

>   No!

>   RAGUENEAU
>   This place is dangerous!—
>   170

CYRANO *(To De Guiche)*
Take her away—I am going—
ROXANE
(Kisses the letter; faintly.)
His blood . . . his tears . . .
RAGUENEAU
(Leaps down from the coach and runs to her.)
She has fainted—
DE GUICHE
(On the parapet; savagely, to the Cadets)
Hold them!
VOICE OFF STAGE
Lay down your arms!
VOICES
No! No!
CYRANO
(To De Guiche)
Sir, you have proved yourself— Take care of her.
DE GUICHE
(Hurries to Roxane and takes her up in his arms.)
As you will—we can win, if you hold on
A little longer—
CYRANO
Good!
*(Calls out to Roxane, as she is carried away, faint-
ing, by De Guiche and Ragueneau.)*
Adieu, Roxane!
*(Tumult, outcries. Several Cadets come back
wounded and fall on the stage. Cyrano, rushing
to the fight, is stopped on the crest of the parapet
by Carbon, covered with blood.)*
CARBON
We are breaking—I am twice wounded—
CYRANO
(Shouts to the Gascons.)
Hardi!
Reculez pas, Drollos!
(To Carbon, holding him up.)
So—never fear!
I have two deaths to avenge now—Christian's
And my own!
*(They come down. Cyrano takes from him the lance
with Roxane's handkerchief still fastened to it.)*
Float, little banner, with her name!

171

> *(He plants it on the parapet; then shouts to the Cadets.)*

Toumbé dessus! Escrasas lous!
> *(To the fifer)*

> Your fife!

Music!

> *(Fife plays. The wounded drag themselves to their feet. Other Cadets scramble over the parapet and group themselves around* CYRANO *and his tiny flag. The coach is filled and covered with men, bristling with muskets, transformed into a redoubt.)*

A CADET

> *(Reels backward over the wall, still fighting. Shouts)*

They are climbing over!—
> *(And falls dead.)*

CYRANO

> Very good—

Let them come!— A salute now—
> *(The parapet is crowned for an instant with a rank of enemies. The imperial banner of Spain is raised aloft.)*

> Fire!

> *(General volley)*

VOICE
> *(Among the ranks of the enemy)*

> Fire!

> *(Murderous counter-fire; the Cadets fall on every side.)*

A SPANISH OFFICER *(Uncovers)*

Who are these men who are so fond of death?

CYRANO
> *(Erect amid the hail of bullets, declaims)*

The Cadets of Gascoyne, the defenders
  Of Carbon de Castel-Jaloux—
Free fighters, free lovers, free spenders—
> *(He rushes forward, followed by a few survivors.)*

The Cadets of Gascoyne . . .
> *(The rest is lost in the din of battle.)*

> *(Curtain)*

THE FIFTH ACT

CYRANO'S GAZETTE

Fifteen years later, in 1655: THE PARK OF THE CONVENT *occupied by the Ladies of the Cross, at Paris.*

Magnificent foliage. To the Left, the House upon a broad Terrace at the head of a flight of steps, with several Doors opening upon the Terrace. In the centre of the scene an enormous Tree alone in the centre of a little open space. Toward the Right, in the foreground, among Boxwood Bushes, a semi-circular Bench of stone.

All the way across the Background of the scene, an Avenue overarched by the chestnut trees, leading to the door of a Chapel on the Right, just visible among the branches of the trees. Beyond the double curtain of the trees, we catch a glimpse of bright lawns and shaded walks, masses of shrubbery; the perspective of the Park; the sky.

A little side door of the Chapel opens upon a Colonnade, garlanded with Autumnal vines, and disappearing on the Right behind the box-trees.

It is late October. Above the still living green of the turf all the foliage is red and yellow and brown. The evergreen masses of Box and Yew stand out darkly against this Autumnal coloring. A heap of dead leaves under every tree. The leaves are falling everywhere. They rustle underfoot along the walks; the Terrace and the Bench are half covered with them.

Before the Bench on the Right, on the side toward the Tree, is placed a tall embroidery frame and beside it a little Chair. Baskets filled with skeins of many-colored silks and balls of wool. Tapestry unfinished on the Frame.

At the CURTAIN RISE *the nuns are coming and going across the Park; several of them are seated on the Bench around* MOTHER MARGUÉRITE DE JÉSUS. *The leaves are falling.*

SISTER MARTHE
(*To* MOTHER MARGUÉRITE)
Sister Claire has been looking in the glass
At her new cap; twice!

MOTHER MARGUÉRITE

(To SISTER CLAIRE*)*

It is very plain;

Very.

SISTER CLAIRE

And Sister Marthe stole a plum
Out of the tart this morning!

MOTHER MARGUÉRITE

(To SISTER MARTHE*)*

That was wrong;

Very wrong.

SISTER CLAIRE

Oh, but such a little look!

SISTER MARTHE

Such a little plum!

MOTHER MARGUÉRITE

(Severely)

I shall tell Monsieur
De Cyrano, this evening.

SISTER CLAIRE

No! Oh, no!—

He will make fun of us.

SISTER MARTHE

He will say nuns

Are so gay!

SISTER CLAIRE

And so greedy!

MOTHER MARGUÉRITE

(Smiling)

And so good . . .

SISTER CLAIRE

It must be ten years, Mother Marguérite,
That he has come here every Saturday,
Is it not?

MOTHER MARGUÉRITE

More than ten years; ever since
His cousin came to live among us here—
Her worldly weeds among our linen veils,
Her widowhood and our virginity—
Like a black dove among white doves.

SISTER MARTHE

No one

Else ever turns that happy sorrow of hers
Into a smile.

ALL THE NUNS

       He is such fun!—He makes us
Almost laugh!—And he teases everyone—
And pleases everyone— And we all love him—
And he likes our cake, too—

SISTER MARTHE

       I am afraid
He is not a good Catholic.

SISTER CLAIRE

      Some day
We shall convert him.

THE NUNS
      Yes—yes!

MOTHER MARGUÉRITE

      Let him be;
I forbid you to worry him. Perhaps
He might stop coming here.

SISTER MARTHE

      But ... God?

MOTHER MARGUÉRITE

      You need not
Be afraid. God knows all about him.

SISTER MARTHE

      Yes ...
But every Saturday he says to me,
Just as if he were proud of it: "Well, Sister,
I ate meat yesterday!"

MOTHER MARGUÉRITE

      He tells you so?
The last time he said that, he had not eaten
Anything, for two days.

SISTER MARTHE

      Mother!—

MOTHER MARGUÉRITE

      He is poor;
Very poor.

SISTER MARTHE
    Who said so?

MOTHER MARGUÉRITE

      Monsieur Le Bret.

SISTER MARTHE
Why does not someone help him?

MOTHER MARGUÉRITE

      He would be
Angry; very angry ...

175

*(Between the trees up stage, ROXANE appears, all
in black, with a widow's cap and long veils. DE
GUICHE, magnificently grown old, walks beside
her. They move slowly. MOTHER MARGUÉRITE
rises.)*

Let us go in—

Madame Madeleine has a visitor.

SISTER MARTHE

(To SISTER CLAIRE)

The Duc de Grammont, is it not? The Marshal?

SISTER CLAIRE

(Looks toward DE GUICHE.)

I think so—yes.

SISTER MARTHE

He has not been to see her

For months—

THE NUNS

He is busy—the Court!—the Camp!—

SISTER CLAIRE

The world! ...

*(They go out. DE GUICHE and ROXANE come down
in silence, and stop near the embroidery frame.
Pause.)*

DE GUICHE

And you remain here, wasting all that gold—
For ever in mourning?

ROXANE

For ever.

DE GUICHE

And still faithful?

ROXANE

And still faithful ...

DE GUICHE

(After a pause)

Have you forgiven me?

ROXANE

(Simply, looking up at the cross of the Convent)

I am here.

(Another pause)

DE GUICHE

Was Christian ... all that?

ROXANE

If you knew him.

DE GUICHE

Ah? We were not precisely ... intimate ...

176

And his last letter—always at your heart?

ROXANE

It hangs here, like a holy reliquary.

DE GUICHE

Dead—and you love him still!

ROXANE

Sometimes I think

He has not altogether died; our hearts
Meet, and his love flows all around me, living.

DE GUICHE

(After another pause)

You see Cyrano often?

ROXANE

Every week.

My old friend takes the place of my Gazette,
Brings me all the news. Every Saturday,
Under that tree where you are now, his chair
Stands, if the day be fine. I wait for him,
Embroidering; the hour strikes; then I hear,
(I need not turn to look!) at the last stroke,
His cane tapping the steps. He laughs at me
For my eternal needlework. He tells
The story of the past week—

(LE BRET appears on the steps.)

There's Le Bret!—

(LE BRET approaches.)

How is it with our friend?

LE BRET

Badly.

DE GUICHE

Indeed?

ROXANE

(To DE GUICHE)

Oh, he exaggerates!

LE BRET

Just as I said—

Loneliness, misery—I told him so!—
His satires make a host of enemies—
He attacks the false nobles, the false saints,
The false heroes, the false artists—in short,
Everyone!

ROXANE

But they fear that sword of his—

No one dare touch him!

(With a shrug)

H'm—that may be so.

LE BRET

It is not violence I fear for him,
But solitude—poverty—old gray December,
Stealing on wolf's feet, with a wolf's green eyes,
Into his darkening room. Those bravoes yet
May strike our Swordsman down! Every day now,
He draws his belt up one hole; his poor nose
Looks like old ivory; he has one coat
Left—his old black serge.

DE GUICHE

That is nothing strange

In this world! No, you need not pity him
Overmuch.

LE BRET

(With a bitter smile)
My lord Marshal! . . .

DE GUICHE

I say, do not

Pity him overmuch. He lives his life,
His own life, his own way—thought, word, and deed
Free!

LE BRET

(As before)
My lord Duke! . . .

DE GUICHE

(Haughtily)

Yes, I know—I have all;

He has nothing. Nevertheless, to-day
I should be proud to shake his hand . . .
(Saluting ROXANE.)

Adieu.

ROXANE

I will go with you.
*(DE GUICHE salutes LE BRET, and turns with ROX-
ANE toward the steps.)*

DE GUICHE

(Pauses on the steps, as she climbs.)
Yes— I envy him

Now and then . . .

Do you know, when a man wins

Everything in this world, when he succeeds
Too much—he feels, having done nothing wrong

Especially, Heaven knows!—he feels somehow
A thousand small displeasures with himself,
Whose whole sum is not quite-Remorse, but rather
A sort of vague disgust . . . The ducal robes
Mounting up, step by step, to pride and power,
Somewhere among their folds draw after them
A rustle of dry illusions, vain regrets,
As your veil, up the stairs here, draws along
The whisper of dead leaves.

ROXANE

(Ironical)

The sentiment

Does you honor.

DE GUICHE

Oh, yes . . .
(Pausing suddenly.)

Monsieur Le Bret!—

(To ROXANE*)*

You pardon us?—
(He goes to LE BRET, *and speaks in a low tone.)*

One moment— It is true

That no one dares attack your friend. Some people
Dislike him, none the less. The other day
At Court, such a one said to me: "This man
Cyrano may die—accidentally."

LE BRET

(Coldly)

Thank you.

DE GUICHE

You may thank me. Keep him at home

All you can. Tell him to be careful.

LE BRET

(Shaking his hands to heaven.)

Careful!—

He is coming here. I'll warn him—yes, but! . . .

ROXANE

(Still on the steps, to a Nun who approaches her)

Here

I am—what is it?

THE NUN

Madame, Ragueneau

Wishes to see you.

ROXANE

Bring him here.

179

(To Le Bret *and* De Guiche*)*

He comes

For sympathy—having been first of all
A Poet, he became since then, in turn,
A Singer—

LE BRET
Bath-house keeper—

ROXANE

Sacristan—

LE BRET

Actor—

ROXANE
Hairdresser—

LE BRET
Music-master—

ROXANE

Now,

To-day—

RAGUENEAU
(Enters hurriedly.)
Madame!—
(He sees Le Bret.*)*

Monsieur!—

ROXANE

(Smiling)

First tell your troubles

To Le Bret for a moment.

RAGUENEAU

But Madame—
(She goes out, with De Guiche, *not hearing him.*
Ragueneau *comes to* Le Bret.*)*

After all, I had rather— You are here—
She need not know so soon— I went to see him
Just now— Our friend— As I came near his door,
I saw him coming out. I hurried on
To join him. At the corner of the street,
As he passed— Could it be an accident?—
I wonder!—At the window overhead,
A lackey with a heavy log of wood
Let it fall—

LE BRET

Cyrano!

RAGUENEAU
I ran to him—
180

God! The cowards!

RAGUENEAU

I found him lying there—

A great hole in his head—

LE BRET

Is he alive?

RAGUENEAU

Alive—yes. But . . . I had to carry him
Up to his room—Dieu! Have you seen his room?—

LE BRET

Is he suffering?

RAGUENEAU

No; unconscious.

LE BRET

Did you

Call a doctor?

RAGUENEAU

One came—for charity.

LE BRET

Poor Cyrano!—We must not tell Roxane
All at once . . . Did the doctor say?—

RAGUENEAU

He said

Fever, and lesions of the— I forget
Those long names— Ah, if you had seen him there,
His head all white bandages!—Let us go
Quickly—there is no one to care for him—
All alone— If he tries to raise his head,
He may die!

LE BRET
(Draws him away to the Right.)

This way— It is shorter—through
The Chapel—

ROXANE
(Appears on the stairway, and calls to Le Bret *as
he is going out by the colonnade which leads to
the small door of the Chapel.)*
Monsieur Le Bret!—
(Le Bret *and* Ragueneau *rush off without
hearing.)*

Running away

When I call to him? Poor dear Ragueneau
Must have been very tragic!

(She comes slowly down the stair, toward the tree.)
                                        What a day! . . .
Something in these bright Autumn afternoons
Happy and yet regretful—an old sorrow
Smiling . . . as though poor little April dried
Her tears long ago—and remembered . . .
            *(She sits down at her work. Two Nuns come out
            of the house carrying a great chair and set it
            under the tree.)*

                                              Ah—

The old chair, for my old friend!—
                    SISTER MARTHE

                                        The best one
In our best parlor!—

                            ROXANE
                    Thank you, Sister—
        (The Nuns withdraw.)

                                              There—
        (She begins embroidering. The clock strikes.)
The hour!—He will be coming now—my silks—
All done striking? He never was so late
Before! The sister at the door—my thimble . . .
Here it is—she must be exhorting him
To repent all his sins . . .
            (A pause)

                                    He ought to be
Converted, by this time— Another leaf—
            *(A dead leaf falls on her work; she brushes it
            away.)*
Certainly nothing could—my scissors—ever
Keep him away—

                        A NUN
            (Appears on the steps.)
                Monsieur de Bergerac.
                        ROXANE
        (Without turning)
What was I saying? . . . Hard, sometimes, to match
These faded colors! . . .
            *(While she goes on working, CYRANO appears at
            the top of the steps, very pale, his hat drawn over
            his eyes. The Nun who has brought him in goes
            away. He begins to descend the steps leaning on
            his cane, and holding himself on his feet only by
            an evident effort. ROXANE turns to him, with a
            tone of friendly banter.)*

After fourteen years,
Late—for the first time!

CYRANO

*(Reaches the chair, and sinks into it; his gay tone
contrasting with his tortured face.)*

Yes, yes—maddening!

I was detained by—

ROXANE

Well?

CYRANO

A visitor,

Most unexpected.

ROXANE

(Carelessly, still sewing)

Was your visitor

Tiresome?

CYRANO

Why, hardly that—inopportune,
Let us say—an old friend of mine—at least
A very old acquaintance.

ROXANE

Did you tell him

To go away?

CYRANO

For the time being, yes.
I said: "Excuse me—this is Saturday—
I have a previous engagement, one
I cannot miss, even for you— Come back
An hour from now."

ROXANE

Your friend will have to wait;
I shall not let you go till dark.

CYRANO *(Very gently)*

Perhaps

A little before dark, I must go . . .

*(He leans back in the chair, and closes his eyes.
SISTER MARTHE crosses above the stairway.
ROXANE sees her, motions her to wait, then turns
to CYRANO.)*

ROXANE

Look—

Somebody waiting to be teased.

CYRANO

(Quickly, opens his eyes.)

Of course!

(In a big, comic voice)

Sister, approach!

> *(SISTER MARTHE glides toward him.)*

> > Beautiful downcast eyes!—

So shy—

SISTER MARTHE

> *(Looks up, smiling.)*
> You—*(She sees his face.)*
> > Oh!—

CYRANO

(Indicates ROXANE.)

> > Sh!—Careful!

(Resumes his burlesque tone.)

> > > Yesterday,

I ate meat again!

SISTER MARTHE

> Yes, I know. *(Aside)*

> > That is why

He looks so pale . . .

> *(To him: low and quickly)*
> > In the refectory,

Before you go—come to me there—

> > I'll make you

A great bowl of hot soup—will you come?

> CYRANO *(Boisterously)*

> > > Ah—

Will I come!

SISTER MARTHE

> You are quite reasonable

To-day!

ROXANE

> Has she converted you?

SISTER MARTHE

> > Oh, no—

Not for the world!—

CYRANO

> > Why, now I think of it,

That is so— You, bursting with holiness,
And yet you never preach! Astonishing
I call it . . .

> *(With burlesque ferocity)*
> > Ah—now I'll astonish you—

I am going to—

> *(With the air of seeking for a good joke and finding it)*

184

                    —let you pray for me
To-night, at vespers!

ROXANE
Aha!

CYRANO
                              Look at her—
Absolutely struck dumb!

SISTER MARTHE
(Gently)
                         I did not wait
For you to say I might. *(She goes out.)*

CYRANO
(Returns to ROXANE, who is bending over her
work.)
                         Now, may the devil
Admire me, if I ever hope to see
The end of that embroidery!

ROXANE *(Smiling)*
                              I thought
It was time you said that.
(A breath of wind causes a few leaves to fall.)

CYRANO
                         The leaves—

ROXANE
(Raises her head and looks away through the trees.)
                              What color—
Perfect Venetian red! Look at them fall.

CYRANO
Yes—they know how to die. A little way
From the branch to the earth, a little fear
Of mingling with the common dust—and yet
They go down gracefully—a fail that seems
Like flying!

ROXANE
Melancholy—you?

CYRANO
                         Why, no,
Roxane!

ROXANE
              Then let the leaves fall. Tell me now
The Court news—my gazette!

CYRANO
                         Let me see—

ROXANE

                                        Ah!

CYRANO
(More and more pale, struggling against pain)

Saturday, the nineteenth; the King fell ill,
After eight helpings of grape marmalade.
His malady was brought before the court,
Found guilty of high treason; whereupon
His Majesty revived. The royal pulse
Is now normal. Sunday, the twentieth:
The Queen gave a grand ball, at which they burned
Seven hundred and sixty-three wax candles. Note:
They say our troops have been victorious
In Austria. Later: Three sorcerers
Have been hung. Special post: The little dog
Of Madame d'Athis was obliged to take
Four pills before—

ROXANE
                    Monsieur de Bergerac,

Will you kindly be quiet!

CYRANO
                              Monday . . . nothing.

Lygdamire has a new lover.

ROXANE
                    Oh!

CYRANO
(His face more and more altered)
                              Tuesday,

The Twenty-second: All the court has gone
To Fontainebleau. Wednesday: The Comte de
    Fiesque
Spoke to Madame de Montglat; she said No.
Thursday: Mancini was the Queen of France
Or—very nearly! Friday: La Montglat
Said Yes. Saturday, twenty-sixth. . . .
(His eyes close; his head sinks back; silence.)

ROXANE
*(Surprised at not hearing any more, turns, looks
    at him, and rises, frightened.)*
                              He has fainted—
(She runs to him, crying out.)
Cyrano!

CYRANO *(Opens his eyes.)*
    What . . . What is it? . . .
(He sees ROXANE *leaning over him, and quickly
    pulls his hat down over his head and leans back
    away from her in the chair.)*

186

It is nothing—truly!

No—oh no—

ROXANE

But—

CYRANO

My old wound—

At Arras—sometimes—you know. . . .

ROXANE

My poor friend!

CYRANO

Oh it is nothing; it will soon be gone. . . .
(Forcing a smile)
There! It is gone!

ROXANE

(Standing close to him)

We all have our old wounds—
I have mine—here . . .
(Her hand at her breast)
under this faded scrap
Of writing. . . . It is hard to read now—all
But the blood—and the tears. . . .
(Twilight begins to fall.)

CYRANO

His letter! . . . Did you
Not promise me that some day . . . that some day. . . .
You would let me read it?

ROXANE

His letter?—You . . .
You wish—

CYRANO

I do wish it—to-day.

ROXANE

(Gives him the little silken bag from around her neck.)

Here. . . .

CYRANO

May I . . . open it?

ROXANE

Open it, and read.
(She goes back to her work, folds it again, rearranges her silks.)

CYRANO

(Unfolds the letter; reads.)
"Farewell Roxane, because to-day I die—"

187

ROXANE *(Looks up, surprised.)*

Aloud?

CYRANO *(Reads)*
"I know that it will be to-day,
My own dearly beloved—and my heart
Still so heavy with love I have not told,
And I die without telling you! No more
Shall my eyes drink the sight of you like wine,
Never more, with a look that is a kiss,
Follow the sweet grace of you—"

ROXANE

How you read it—

His letter!

CYRANO *(Continues)*
"I remember now the way
You have, of pushing back a lock of hair
With one hand, from your forehead—and my heart
Cries out—"

ROXANE

His letter . . . and you read it so . . .
(The darkness increases imperceptibly.)

CYRANO
"Cries out and keeps crying: 'Farewell, my dear,
My dearest—'"

ROXANE

In a voice. . . .

CYRANO

"—My own heart's own,
My own treasure—"

ROXANE *(Dreamily)*
In such a voice. . . .

CYRANO

—"My love—"

ROXANE

—As I remember hearing . . .
(She trembles.)

—long ago. . . .

*(She comes near him, softly, without his seeing her;
passes the chair, leans over silently, looking at the
letter. The darkness increases.)*

CYRANO
"—I am never away from you. Even now,
I shall not leave you. In another world,
I shall be still that one who loves you, loves you
Beyond measure, beyond—"

188

ROXANE

(Lays her hand on his shoulder.)

How can you read
Now? It is dark. . . .

*(He starts, turns, and sees her there close to him.
A little movement of surprise, almost of fear; then
he bows his head.*

*A long pause; then in the twilight now completely
fallen, she says very softly, clasping her hands)*

And all these fourteen years,
He has been the old friend, who came to me
To be amusing.

CYRANO

Roxane !—

ROXANE

It was you.

CYRANO

No, no, Roxane, no !

ROXANE

And I might have known,
Every time that I heard you speak my name ! . . .

CYRANO

No— It was not I—

ROXANE

It was . . . you !

CYRANO

I swear—

ROXANE

I understand everything now : The letters—
That was you . . .

CYRANO

No !

ROXANE

And the dear, foolish words—
That was you. . . .

CYRANO

No !

ROXANE

And the voice . . . in the dark. . . .
That was . . . you !

CYRANO

On my honor—

ROXANE

And . . . the Soul !—
That was all you.

189

CYRANO

I never loved you—

ROXANE

Yes,

You loved me.

CYRANO *(Desperately)*

No— He loved you—

ROXANE

Even now,

You love me!

CYRANO *(His voice weakens.)*

No!

ROXANE *(Smiling)*

And why . . . so great a "No"?

CYRANO

No, no, my own dear love, I love you not! . . .
(Pause)

ROXANE

How many things have died . . . and are newborn! . . .
Why were you silent for so many years,
All the while, every night and every day,
He gave me nothing—you knew that— You knew
Here, in this letter lying on my breast,
Your tears— You knew they were your tears—

CYRANO

(Holds the letter out to her.)

The blood

Was his.

ROXANE

Why do you break that silence now,
To-day?

CYRANO

Why? Oh, because—
(LE BRET and RAGUENEAU enter, running.)

LE BRET

What recklessness—

I knew it! He is here!

CYRANO

(Smiling, and trying to rise)

Well? Here I am!

RAGUENEAU

He has killed himself, Madame, coming here!

ROXANE

He— Oh, God. . . . And that faintness . . . was that?—

190

No,

Nothing! I did not finish my Gazette—
Saturday, twenty-sixth: An hour or so
Before dinner, Monsieur de Bergerac
Died, foully murdered.

> *(He uncovers his head, and shows it swathed in bandages.)*

ROXANE

Oh, what does he mean?—

Cyrano!— What have they done to you?—

CYRANO

"Struck down

By the sword of a hero, let me fall—
Steel in my heart, and laughter on my lips!"
Yes, I said that once. How Fate loves a jest!—
Behold me ambushed—taken in the rear—
My battlefield a gutter—my noble foe
A lackey, with a log of wood! . . .

It seems

Too logical— I have missed everything,
Even my death!

RAGUENEAU *(Breaks down.)*

Ah, monsieur!—

CYRANO

Ragueneau,

Stop blubbering! *(Takes his hand.)*

What are you writing nowadays,

Old poet?

RAGUENEAU *(Through his tears)*

I am not a poet now;
I snuff the—light the candles—for Molière!

CYRANO

Oh—Molière!

RAGUENEAU

Yes, but I am leaving him

To-morrow. Yesterday they played "Scapin"—
He has stolen your scene—

LE BRET

The whole scene—word for word!

RAGUENEAU

Yes: "What the devil was he doing there"—
That one!

LE BRET *(Furious)*
And Molière stole it all from you—

Bodily!—

CYRANO
Bah— He showed good taste. . . .
(To RAGUENEAU*)*

The Scene

Went well? . . .

RAGUENEAU
Ah, monsieur, they laughed—and laughed—
How they did laugh!

CYRANO
Yes—that has been my life. . . .
Do you remember that night Christian spoke
Under your window? It was always so!
While I stood in the darkness underneath,
Others climbed up to win the applause—the kiss!—
Well—that seems only justice— I still say,
Even now, on the threshold of my tomb—
"Molière has genius—Christian had good looks—"

*(The chapel bell is ringing. Along the avenue of
trees above the stairway, the Nuns pass in procession to their prayers.)*

They are going to pray now; there is the bell.

ROXANE
(Raises herself and calls to them)
Sister!—Sister!—

CYRANO *(Holding on to her hand)*
No,—do not go away—
I may not still be here when you return. . . .

*(The Nuns have gone into the chapel. The organ
begins to play.)*

A little harmony is all I need—
Listen. . . .

ROXANE
You shall not die! I love you!—

CYRANO

No—

That is not in the story! You remember
When Beauty said "I love you" to the Beast
That was a fairy prince, his ugliness
Changed and dissolved, like magic. . . . But you see
I am still the same.

ROXANE
And I—I have done

192

This to you! All my fault—mine!

CYRANO

You? Why no,

On the contrary! I had never known
Womanhood and its sweetness but for you.
My mother did not love to look at me—
I never had a sister— Later on,
I feared the mistress with a mockery
Behind her smile. But you—because of you
I have had one friend not quite all a friend—
Across my life, one whispering silken gown! . . .

LE BRET

*(Points to the rising moon which begins to shine
down between the trees.)*

Your other friend is looking at you.

CYRANO *(Smiling at the moon)*

I see. . . .

ROXANE

I never loved but one man in my life,
And I have lost him—twice. . . .

CYRANO

Le Bret—I shall be up there presently
In the moon—without having to invent
Any flying machines!

ROXANE

What are you saying? . . .

CYRANO

The moon—yes, that would be the place for me—
My kind of paradise! I shall find there
Those other souls who should be friends of mine—
Socrates—Galileo—

LE BRET *(Revolting)*

No! No! No!

It is too idiotic—too unfair—
Such a friend—such a poet—such a man
To die so—to die so!—

CYRANO *(Affectionately)*

There goes Le Bret,

Growling!

LE BRET *(Breaks down.)*

My friend!—

CYRANO

(Half raises himself, his eye wanders.)

The Cadets of Gascoyne,

The Defenders. . . . The elementary mass—

Ah—there's the point! Now, then . . .

LE BRET

Delirious—

And all that learning—

CYRANO

On the other hand,

We have Copernicus—

ROXANE

Oh!

CYRANO

(More and more delirious)

"Very well,
But what the devil was he doing there?—
What the devil was he doing there, up there?" . . .

(He declaims)

Philosopher and scientist,
Poet, musician, duellist—
He flew high, and fell back again!
A pretty wit—whose like we lack—
A lover . . . not like other men. . . .
Here lies Hercule-Savinien
De Cyrano de Bergerac—
Who was all things—and all in vain!

Well, I must go—pardon— I cannot stay!
My moonbeam comes to carry me away. . . .

(He falls back into the chair, half fainting. The sobbing of ROXANE *recalls him to reality. Gradually his mind comes back to him. He looks at her, stroking the veil that hides her hair.)*

I would not have you mourn any the less
That good, brave, noble Christian; but perhaps—
I ask you only this—when the great cold
Gathers around my bones, that you may give
A double meaning to your widow's weeds
And the tears you let fall for him may be
For a little—my tears. . . .

ROXANE (Sobbing)

Oh, my love! . . .

CYRANO

(Suddenly shaken as with a fever fit, he raises himself erect and pushes her away.)

—Not here!—

Not lying down! . . .

(They spring forward to help him; he motions them back.)

Let no one help me—no one !—
Only the tree. . . .

(He sets his back against the trunk. Pause.)

It is coming . . . I feel
Already shod with marble . . . gloved with lead . . .
(Joyously)
Let the old fellow come now ! He shall find me
On my feet—sword in hand—*(Draws his sword.)*

LE BRET

Cyrano !—

ROXANE *(Half fainting)*

Oh,
Cyrano !

CYRANO

I can see him there—he grins—
He is looking at my nose—that skeleton
—What's that you say ? Hopeless ?—Why, very well !—
But a man does not fight merely to win !
No—no—better to know one fights in vain ! . . .
You there— Who are you ? A hundred against one—
I know them now, my ancient enemies—
(He lunges at the empty air.)
Falsehood ! . . . There ! There ! Prejudice— Compromise—
Cowardice—*(Thrusting)*

What's that ? No ! Surrender ? No !
Never—never ! . . .

Ah, you too, Vanity !
I knew you would overthrow me in the end—
No ! I fight on ! I fight on ! I fight on !
*(He swings the blade in great circles, then pauses,
gasping. When he speaks again, it is in another
tone.)*
Yes, all my laurels you have riven away
And all my roses ; yet in spite of you,
There is one crown I bear away with me,
And to-night, when I enter before God,
My salute shall sweep all the stars away
From the blue threshold ! One thing without stain,
Unspotted from the world, in spite of doom
Mine own !—
(He springs forward, his sword aloft.)
And that is . . .
*(The sword escapes from his hand ; he totters, and
falls into the arms of LE BRET and RAGUENEAU.)*

195

ROXANE

(Bends over him and kisses him on the forehead.)

—That is . . .

CYRANO

(Opens his eyes and smiles up at her.)

My white plume. . . .

(Curtain)

Bantam Classics bring you the world's greatest literature—books that have stood the test of time—at specially low prices. These beautifully designed books will be proud additions to your bookshelf. You'll want all these time-tested classics for your own reading pleasure.

☐	21137	**PERSUASION** Jane Austen	$2.95
☐	21051	**DAVID COPPERFIELD** Charles Dickens	$2.50
☐	21148	**DRACULA** Bram Stoker	$1.95
☐	21044	**FRANKENSTEIN** Mary Shelley	$1.50
☐	21171	**ANNA KARENINA** Leo Tolstoy	$2.95
☐	21035	**THE DEATH OF IVAN ILYICH** Leo Tolstoy	$1.95
☐	21163	**THE BROTHERS KARAMAZOV** Fyodor Dostoevsky	$2.95
☐	21175	**CRIME AND PUNISHMENT** Fyodor Dostoevsky	$2.50
☐	21136	**THE IDIOT** Fyodor Dostoevsky	$3.50
☐	21166	**CANDIDE** Voltaire	$2.25
☐	21187	**THE COUNT OF MONTE CRISTO** Alexandre Dumas	$3.50
☐	21118	**CYRANO DE BERGERAC** Edmond Rostand	$1.75
☐	21048	**SILAS MARNER** George Eliot	$1.75
☐	21089	**FATHERS AND SONS** Ivan Turgenev	$1.95
☐	21032	**THE HUNCHBACK OF NOTRE DAME** Victor Hugo	$1.95
☐	21101	**MADAME BOVARY** Gustave Flaubert	$2.50
☐	21059	**THE TURN OF THE SCREW AND OTHER SHORT FICTION** Henry James	$1.95

Bantam Classics bring you the world's greatest literature—books that have stood the test of time—at specially low prices. These beautifully designed books
will be proud additions to your bookshelf. You'll
want all these time-tested classics for your own
reading pleasure.

Titles by *Charles Dickens*

☐ 21123	**THE PICKWICK PAPERS**	$4.95
☐ 21108	**BLEAK HOUSE**	$3.95
☐ 21086	**NICHOLAS NICKLEBY**	$4.50
☐ 21189	**DAVID COPPERFIELD**	$3.50
☐ 21113	**GREAT EXPECTATIONS**	$2.50
☐ 21106	**A TALE OF TWO CITIES**	$1.95
☐ 21016	**HARD TIMES**	$1.95

Titles by *Thomas Hardy:*

☐ 21152	**JUDE THE OBSCURE**	$2.75
☐ 21024	**THE MAYOR OF CASTERBRIDGE**	$1.95
☐ 21080	**THE RETURN OF THE NATIVE**	$1.95
☐ 21168	**TESS OF THE D'URBERVILLES**	$2.95
☐ 21131	**FAR FROM THE MADDENING CROWD**	$2.75

☐ 21059	**THE TURN OF THE SCREW AND OTHER SHORT FICTION** Henry James	$1.95
☐ 21021	**WUTHERING HEIGHTS** Emily Brontë	$1.75
☐ 21149	**LADY CHATTERLEY'S LOVER** D. H. Lawrence	$2.75
☐ 21159	**EMMA** Jane Austen	$1.95

Prices and availability subject to change without notice.

Buy them at your local bookstore or use this handy coupon for ordering:

Bantam Books, Inc., Dept. CL3, 414 East Golf Road, Des Plaines, Ill. 60016

Please send me the books I have checked above. I am enclosing $_____
(please add $1.25 to cover postage and handling). Send check or money order
—no cash or C.O.D.'s please.

Mr/Mrs/Miss _____

Address_____

City_____ State/Zip_____

CL3—3/85

Please allow four to six weeks for delivery. This offer expires 9/85.

These books have been bestsellers for generations of readers. Bantam Classics now bring you the world's greatest literature in specially low-priced editions. From the American epic Moby Dick to Dostoevsky's towering works, you'll want all these time-tested classics for your own.